PENGUIN BOOKS

SWIM, BIKE, RUN

'Incredible brothers. Provides an authentic account of what it takes to be great' *Scotsman*

'In one of the most dramatic episodes of the Olympics, Alistair and Jonny Brownlee secured a place in British sporting history – and legend status in their native Yorkshire. The producers of *Chariots of Fire* have their twenty-first-century sequel on a plate' *Daily Mail*

'There is a golden rule in triathlon: when a Brownlee races, they win. They are incredibly close, do most things together, train as a team and yet come the big race they are deadly rivals' *Guardian*

'Under the pressure of the biggest race of their lives, they delivered in unforgettable style' *Daily Telegraph*

'A fast-paced, candid, enjoyable book that could as equally be devoured by a wide-eyed sporty teen as a hardcore endurance junkie' *TriRadar*

'A fascinating, well-written and surprisingly funny account of the Brownlee brothers' formative years, training, key races and relationship' *Tri247*

'Sport has two new heroes: a couple of nice lads from Yorkshire' *The Times*

ABOUT THE AUTHORS

Alistair Brownlee, twenty-six, is a British triathlete from Yorkshire. He is the reigning Olympic champion, a back-to-back European champion and a two-time world champion.

Jonathan Brownlee, twenty-four, is also a British triathlete from Yorkshire. He is a two-time world sprint champion, an Olympic bronze medalist and the 2013 world champion.

Tom Fordyce is the BBC's Chief Sports Writer. A keen amateur triathlete and runner, he is the author of two books, *We Could Be Heroes* and *Karma Chameleons*.

Swim, Bike, Run

Our Triathlon Story

ALISTAIR BROWNLEE AND
JONATHAN BROWNLEE

with Tom Fordyce

PENGUIN BOOKS

PENGUIN BOOKS

Published by the Penguin Group
Penguin Books Ltd, 80 Strand, London WC2R 0RL, England
Penguin Group (USA) Inc., 375 Hudson Street, New York, New York 10014, USA
Penguin Group (Canada), 90 Eglinton Avenue East, Suite 700, Toronto, Ontario, Canada M4P 2Y3
(a division of Pearson Penguin Canada Inc.)
Penguin Ireland, 25 St Stephen's Green, Dublin 2, Ireland (a division of Penguin Books Ltd)
Penguin Group (Australia), 707 Collins Street, Melbourne, Victoria 3008, Australia
(a division of Pearson Australia Group Pty Ltd)
Penguin Books India Pvt Ltd, 11 Community Centre, Panchsheel Park, New Delhi – 110 017, India
Penguin Group (NZ), 67 Apollo Drive, Rosedale, Auckland 0632, New Zealand
(a division of Pearson New Zealand Ltd)
Penguin Books (South Africa) (Pty) Ltd, Block D, Rosebank Office Park,
181 Jan Smuts Avenue, Parktown North, Gauteng 2193, South Africa

Penguin Books Ltd, Registered Offices: 80 Strand, London WC2R 0RL, England

www.penguin.com

First published by Viking 2013
Published in Penguin Books 2014
001

Typeset by Jouve (UK), Milton Keynes
Printed in Great Britain by Clays Ltd, St Ives plc

ISBN: 978-0-241-96584-9

www.greenpenguin.co.uk

To Mum and Dad,
for everything they have done.

CONTENTS

Prologue

ALISTAIR BROWNLEE

Six forty-five a.m., 7 August 2012. I opened my eyes and looked around.

I saw the ceiling of my hotel room. I saw piles of kit strewn around the floor. I sat up in bed and asked myself how I felt.

How do you sleep the night before a home Olympic final, the biggest two hours of your life?

If you're me, the answer – rather unusually – was extremely well.

Two nights earlier I just couldn't get down. I had turned the light off, lain there for half an hour, turned it back on again to read, and then repeated the whole cycle. But with the hooter in London's Hyde Park just hours away, I had no such problems, nodding off around ten p.m. and then waking up nine hours later, completely naturally. I had only one thought: where did the time go?

Instantly I felt the excitement. Never before have I felt like that on the morning of a race; usually there are nerves. You are shaky, you struggle to eat breakfast. This morning there was none of that. It was pure excitement.

JONNY BROWNLEE

I looked out of my hotel-room window. Blue skies, a few white clouds. There would be no torrential rain, as there had been all summer. But there would be no heatwave either. Normal British summer weather. Good.

When your race starts close to midday you don't want to eat breakfast too early. So I turned on BBC *Breakfast* news, and there it was: a reporter doing a preview for the nation, standing on the race finish line, the Serpentine in the background, Union flags fluttering in the foreground, all of it less than a mile away from where I sat.

For once this didn't trigger the nerves I would normally feel. Instead there was a delightful thrill. Wow! It's actually here!

There was little to do but count off the minutes. As always my kit was already packed. My bottles were ready. My energy gels were in place. Our bikes were taken care of; our wetsuits were taken care of.

With an hour and a half before the start we strolled across into Hyde Park and into the athletes' entrance, completely at ease, completely unaware of the madness that was going on everywhere else.

Even at that early stage, Hyde Park was in glorious ferment. There were spectators ten-deep around the bike course, thirty-deep around the Serpentine. People were hanging out of trees. But because we were entering through a cordoned-off area, we saw almost no one. This is rather disappointing, I thought. Where are the crowds?

The home-town support that had defined London's splendid Olympics so far, and would define that day too, became obvious in small stages. We arrived at the main security check-point on our bikes.

'All right, lads?' said the army boys on duty. 'You lads ride straight through.' Alarms were sounding. Our rucksacks were on our bikes, unopened and unchecked. 'Keep going, lads,' they told us. 'Don't you worry about that.' Just behind us were the

French team. 'Right, you lot. Off your bikes. Open your bags.' Brilliant.

As we set up our helmets and running shoes in the transition area – which we would later come sprinting into after the swim and then the cycle – we became aware of the thousands crammed in along the banks of the Serpentine. Then, coming round a corner and out from behind a screen as we headed out on our bikes for a brief warm-up, the noise hit us.

Bang! It was incredible, almost disconcerting. What should we do – wave? Smile? Try to acknowledge it all?

At a stroke any final nerves went. I looked at the endless smiling faces, felt the cheers hammering my ears and thought: this is the coolest thing I've ever experienced.

ALISTAIR

The noise was impossible to imagine. We would find out afterwards that lots of mates who had driven down from Yorkshire at dawn that morning couldn't even get close to a vantage point – some managed to find a spot by one of the two giant screens, but some had to turn right round and drive home again.

Of course, we were oblivious to all this, locked into the last countdown before the show began. We checked transition, checked our positions, checked our slots on the starting pontoon. This was our mantra: 'It's an ordinary race in Hyde Park, racing the same rivals, wearing familiar kit.'

And so to the pontoon. We were announced to waves of cheers rolling across the Serpentine from all sides. It had clouded over now, warm but not scorching, the water cold enough, at 19 °C, for wetsuits to be mandatory. As strong swimmers we always prefer a non-wetsuit swim – they give weaker swimmers a decent boost – but we had expected this, and we had prepared for it.

We jogged to our positions on the extreme right. Water splashed on the face, green swim-hat pulled tight, goggles lowered on to eyes and adjusted.

A helicopter clattering overhead. Heart thumping.

Twenty-four years, all building up to this. Eighteen years of training, much of it brutal, much of it wonderful, culminating in this single race.

Mum and Dad on the lakeside, barely able to look. Old swim coaches and young training partners gathered round their televisions. Best mates in the grandstand, thousands squeezed in tight along the loops and turns of the course, most of Yorkshire and millions around the world watching, waiting, wondering.

Into a crouch, poised for the hooter. Three. Two. One . . .

Learning the Game

ALISTAIR

My mum, Cathy, will tell you that I was always an energetic young Brownlee. I'd keep her awake during pregnancy by kicking in the womb. When she finally got off to sleep, my dad's pager would invariably beep (Keith was a doctor, on call), and that would be it – more movement, less sleep. In utero as in adulthood.

From what my parents say, I was a challenging first child, wriggling, demanding, never still for a second. They loved to go on walks through the Yorkshire Dales north of our home in Horsforth, just outside Leeds, so I would be placed in a papoose and one of them would carry me on their chest. All other babies were happy to lie facing in, snug and protected. Not me. I would squirm and squeal until I was facing outwards, staring back at the world. It got Mum into trouble – 'Don't you know your baby's facing the wrong way?' 'Don't you know you could hurt that poor thing?' I'm not sure there was much she could do about it.

By eight months old I was walking. By two I was talking fluently, embarrassing Mum by asking her strange questions when she was at the till in the supermarket. There was an obsession with reading, and an apparent ability to recall every single one of my Ladybird books from cover to cover. Even when it was filthy outside I wanted to be out there, running round the garden at home, digging holes, mucking about. Mum reckoned that I needed to be outside for at least two hours a day or she wouldn't be able to get me to sleep come bedtime. I hope she is exaggerating when she says I'd have needed Ritalin if I hadn't discovered swimming, but maybe that's not far off the mark.

I can remember waiting for Jonny to be born. I was in the garden, digging a hole for my cars, just after my second birthday. As soon as he was old enough to cope with it I started pushing him round the house and garden in a little trolley, which I like to think ignited his interest in bikes.

A couple of years after he arrived we moved into the house in Horsforth that my parents still live in. That meant we would grow up in separate bedrooms, but we would always play together. We'd mess about in the street, mess about in the garden, play football, build dams in the river. I don't think I so much bossed him about as dragged him around.

JONNY

I would deny this vehemently, but Dad says that, as a little boy, I worshipped my big brother. When he first went off to nursery, leaving me as an eight-month-old at home, I crawled round the house in search of him for so long and so far that my knees bled.

If that story hardly shows me in a flattering light, Mum then tells me that I had almost no self-confidence. I was far more timid than Alistair had been. That's where she thinks my obsession with planning began, to make sure I was never left alone or helpless.

My parents have video tapes of Alistair pushing me round on the little trolley he had, round the house and round the garden, and of me falling off and bumping my head on walls. To him I was something of a toy. My earliest memory of him is when my parents moved to the house we grew up in. I can't picture what he looked like, but I can remember wanting to have the room next to him. I was two years old, and my only thought was: I'm next to Alistair so it will be okay now.

We did everything together. It was rare for us to fall out. When we did, it involved fighting for sporting supremacy of one kind or another: whose turn it was to play table tennis in the back garden, who was next on the climbing frame. I once hit Alistair over the head with a golf club, although I have no recollection of why I did it; I remember only the instant fear of recrimination and retribution.

Our little brother Ed arrived when I was five and Alistair was seven. As Ed got older Alistair and I would fall out a little more, because now there was an ally to call on or recruit. But we never had periods of not talking to each other, or refusing to play.

ALISTAIR

You know how it is with siblings – each of you has a burning sense of injustice founded on the idea that your parents like the other one more, or will side with the other one when it comes to arguments. 'Mum, Jonny's done . . .' would be greeted with, 'Alistair, what have you done to Jonny?' I was always in the wrong, apparently, although Dad will accuse me of paranoia if I mention it today.

My parents like reminding me of one story of when Jonny was two years old and standing up in his cot in the bedroom. There was wallpaper everywhere – on the floor, stuck to his face, stuck to his hands. My mum looked at him, aghast. 'Jonny, what have you done to the wallpaper?' He looked back at her and said, 'Alistair did it.' All lies, of course.

My dad will tell you that I was a very self-assured and confident little boy. I can't remember this, but at his mum's sister's wedding, I was the page boy, all dressed up in a sailor suit (maybe that's why I've wiped it from my memory). I was barely old enough to walk, but I marched up the aisle with no fear whatsoever, having been told only once what was expected of me.

JONNY

The origin of our sporting genes is something of a family dispute. Mum used to swim when she was younger. Breaststroke was her forte, and she swam a few times for Wales, although because Granddad was in the armed forces she was actually born in Penang. Plan B, therefore, was for her to try to represent Malaysia. Dad is from Cleveland and he ran for his county. But they went into medicine as students and the sport was soon dropped.

Our granddad on our dad's side, Norm from Hartlepool, is always telling us we have him to thank for where we are today. There are a few reasons. First, he claims one of his relatives was a national pole-vault champion. We've never been able to verify this part of the story. Secondly, during the war his father, Archibald, was in the merchant navy. The ship he was crewing was sunk, and he managed to swim to shore. Norm states that the fact his father was fit enough to swim to safety proves that our own swimming abilities come directly from him. He also says he has always been the fittest man he knows, on the basis that he walks five miles every morning. When he sees other people walking he insists they're copying his own excellent example.

ALISTAIR

Every time Norm sees me he says the same thing: 'You really remind me of someone. Yeah, you remind me of me, actually.'

Sport and exercise were always around us. Mum and Dad

loved walking; Dad would cycle; Mum would swim. Our other granddad loved swimming, and was always keen to take us to the pool for fun, or lessons and galas.

I was first taken swimming as a toddler, and, unlike Jonny a few years later, I really enjoyed it – I was enrolled in the local council scheme and I quickly worked my way up through the levels. By the age of three and a half I had my first taste of racing – against Dad, in the sea off the Bedruthan Steps Hotel in Cornwall in September 1991. I think it ended in an honourable draw.

Jonny used to hate it and Mum would have to drag him to the pool. He hid his swimming bag so he wouldn't have to go.

JONNY

At playgroup I cried all the time. And I would refuse to let Mum leave me at friends' birthday parties, because I was scared that there would be no one to help me cut up my pizza.

Flattering stuff, isn't it? It gets better. When I was four years old and first taken to swimming lessons, at Holt Park leisure centre in Cookridge, there was a huge guy with dreadlocks at the pool who inadvertently terrified me. I was so scared of this man that I'd refuse to get in the water unless I could see Mum at all times. She would have to stand behind the glass wall in my full sight until I'd forgotten that I was scared. Only when Alistair was in the next lane would I relax a little more. When we later moved up to the City of Leeds club sessions, I could just about handle it because the lady who would help coach us was nice, and I trusted her.

So my swimming career did not begin well, but I went through the Dolphins scheme: bronze and silver and gold. The scheme began with splashing about and being told to do froggy legs. From there to the Olympic podium seems like a long way, but all journeys start somewhere.

Having Alistair around me, swimming or not, was always a source of comfort. We started at Richmond House School at the same time – me in the nursery, Alistair in the infants – and I soon learned how to use him to help me out.

We lived most of those days outdoors. Our grandparents owned a tiny cottage up in Coverdale, tucked in on the south side of Wensleydale in the Yorkshire Dales. It was a basic place – the two of us and, later, little brother Ed all crammed into one bedroom, one on the top bunk, one down below and one on a mattress on the floor. There was a fire which heated the water and a supply of coal in the shed to keep it all going.

Alistair learned to walk on the gate of the Methodist chapel there, and both of us pushed our physical boundaries in those Dales from that point on. There was no back garden, but there were miles of empty countryside all around and a big lake at Semerwater, where we could swim and sail. The cycling was fantastic, tiny roads snaking out from the hamlet into the fells and fields. The ride from the cottage up to Tan Hill and the highest pub in England was a favourite for both of us.

We'd take a little boat out on to Semerwater, Al trying to capsize it, me getting so sick of him trying that I would just jump in and swim back to the shore. Even at Easter, when the water was still freezing, we'd be in there in our wetsuits, swimming out and round the buoy.

Mum and Dad's attitude seemed to be that we should try everything. It meant there were scrapes – like the time I was trying to stand on a windsurfing board, despite being only six years old, and I got caught by a gust of wind which carried me a quarter of a mile out into the lake. But it made us appreciate that we were capable of far more than we thought.

ALISTAIR

Mum and Dad were always happy to indulge my independent streak, the desire to do it all myself. If I couldn't work something out on my own, my attitude was that it couldn't be worth knowing. At an age when most kids aren't even walking home from school alone I was disappearing off into the Dales on long solo bike rides, refusing Dad's offer of his mobile phone in case I got lost; I would just take a quick glance at the map on the way out and tell them breezily that I could remember it all.

When I was nine, Dad took me to my first Leeds Schools Cross Country Championships – 450 entrants, no age categories, and me three years younger than the big lads. I finished 400th.

Dad said I was bright red in the face. The part he considers more significant came in the car as we sat there after the race trying to warm up. 'I think I'm a bit tubby for a runner,' I told him. 'I think I'll stop eating chips and puddings.' And I did. I switched to boiled potatoes and fruit, although it wasn't long until I changed my mind.

I did my first-ever duathlon in east Leeds at the age of nine. It was no big deal – just something I'd spotted up on the noticeboard at the City of Leeds swimming club where we trained at that time.

The swim part of it was fine. It was the run where things started to go wrong: within a hundred metres my shoe came off. These were not nice streets – there was broken glass all over the place, grit, gravel, dog mess – you name it. Mum and Dad were shouting at me to stop, but there was no way that was happening. I kept going, minus one shoe, and made it all the way round. With feet that were blistered and bleeding.

I loved every second of it.

My first-ever triathlon was the Nottingham Children's race in 1997, still aged nine. There was no great thought that I was going to be a triathlete – I just liked the idea of a race where you could do three of my favourite things in a row. My uncle Simon was into the sport, and I'd been to watch him race at Ilkley. I knew what triathlon was, and I knew I might like it.

I was using a bike that was several years too big for me, and I fell off it four times as I tried to get started, but I was always going to carry on. I didn't win; I didn't get anywhere close. But I came back the following year and won the National Series, aged ten. The name of the kid who won the under-eight category? Brownlee. Jonny Brownlee.

I hated the idea of anything stopping me exercising. It didn't matter if it was freezing outside, if there was horizontal sleet battering against the windows and tea almost on the table. I'd stick on my vest and shorts and head out for a run anyway.

Aged ten I decided I wanted to get up early for an extra run before school, out round Horsforth woods. I would set my alarm clock for six thirty, jump out of bed, wake up Dad and force him to come with me. Dad, being less keen on such early starts, would wait until I was asleep and then sneak into my room to turn the alarm off. But, being determined to get my run in, I would then hide the alarm clock so he was unable to switch it off. I won.

I was such a small boy for my age that Mum and Dad couldn't possibly have imagined I would ever be a professional sportsman. But there were symptoms appearing everywhere.

In swimming lessons at the City of Leeds club I would start each term at the back of the lane. A week in, I'd be fast enough to be moved to the front. I had a friend whose father had been a pro rugby player. He took Mum aside once and said that I would make it. She thought he was bonkers. 'What, that skinny little thing?'

The same thing happened again when I was twelve, and running my first 800 metre race for Bingley Harriers. I came last. But an old boy watching from the home straight came up to Mum afterwards and said, with absolute certainty, that I would one day become a great runner. He told her that he'd seen several kids develop into great runners, and that I was another. To this day Mum has no idea who he was, but within a few years she was forced to start believing him.

JONNY

I was dragged into sport because of Alistair. Had he not been swimming, I'm sure I would never have stuck at it. My memories of those lessons are not particularly fond. I asked my parents about this before the Olympics – I thought the sessions were two and a half hours long. It turns out I was exaggerating by an hour. But I was only seven, and at that age it was genuinely hard. At one session you had to swim a full length underwater, kicking only, before you were allowed to get out. I tried and tried, but I just couldn't do it. I was still trying long after everyone else had left.

Those sessions were on a Sunday evening and affected the entire day. Wherever we were, whatever we were doing, at three p.m. it would all have to be sacrificed. Arguably it was too much for a kid of my age. Equally, that's the stuff that makes you strong. Why did I keep going? Because Alistair did, and because my parents made me. The logic was simple: Alistair's going, so we're all going. There's no point in you just sitting there and watching him do it. They couldn't leave me in the house on my own because I was too young. If I'd been closer in age to Edward maybe I would have played around with him instead, but I had no choice.

When my parents forced me to do something, I invariably wanted to do the opposite. Alistair showed quite a lot of promise at music. Later on he would become good enough to reach grade seven at singing and grade six with the flute. None of that rubbed off on me. I chose to take up piano lessons; but I ended up hating them so much that I would wrap my fingers in toilet paper and tell the teacher that I'd broken them, and so had been unable to practise. When I discovered my parents' bountiful medical supplies – one of the great advantages of having doctors for parents – I stole bandages and did an even more convincing job. That piano teacher must have thought I was the most injury-prone child in Yorkshire. Every week, another digit broken.

I found I was far better at team sports. I got pretty good at football, good enough in my early teens to be spotted by coaches from Leeds United, at which point my mum told them not to be so stupid. Couldn't they see that I was too small? Despite her faint praise I would go on to skipper the school rugby team and play for the cricket first eleven. Alistair was hopeless at any sport that required coordination. He tried gymnastics, and was the most awkward kid in the hall; then, in his only recorded game of cricket, he spent his time making daisy chains on the boundary and completely failed to see the ball the only time it came anywhere near him.

But it was Alistair's influence that got me to try my first triathlon, aged eight. As he got better the influence grew stronger. At a point when all I wanted to do was play football or rugby, the fact that he was bringing home cool free kit – T-shirts, bike jerseys, tri-suits, then these incredible bikes – got me thinking: wow, I want to be part of that. That he was always training made it far easier for me to go as well. He found the run routes, he found the training groups. And he was always there to train with.

Sometimes, if you're forced to do stuff, you want to do the opposite. When my parents stopped forcing me to swim, bike and run, that's when I wanted to do them again.

ALISTAIR

So many things had to fall into place for us to end up where we are today. So many other things had to not happen. When I look back and talk to Mum and Dad about those strange little pivots, one example stands out.

Jonny and I were playing in a stream in the middle of Coverdale, near to the cottage, building a dam. Jonny yelled and pulled his finger out of the river, and suddenly it was pouring blood – loads of it was gushing out, Mum was screaming, all hell was breaking loose. We had to rush him to hospital, and the nearest one with an A&E department was Northallerton.

While Jonny was having surgery, Dad got chatting to a few of the staff. An hour later he was being offered a job there. For a while it looked like he was going to take up their offer. If he had, it would have been goodbye Horsforth, hello Northallerton. Had we moved there we couldn't have got our hard-core swimming in because there wouldn't have been a swimming club; we would have been at a small school without a competitive running club; there wouldn't have been a cycling club. In one swoop we'd have lost everything that took us into triathlon, and all because of a bleeding finger.

JONNY

For all that our parents gave us with their love of exercise and of the outdoors, our futures in sport were moulded by a colourful cast of characters that existed around the Leeds area as we grew up. Some were eccentric, others obsessive, and each of them, in their own way, was integral to the formation of the people and athletes we have become.

ALISTAIR

Our school and its teachers could not have been better for us. Even the geographical position of Bradford Grammar in relation to our home in Horsforth was perfect, because we could cycle pretty much all the way there along the canal from our house. It was ten miles, or forty minutes of hard pedalling, which meant it was an ideal training session for us without being so far that we would arrive exhausted.

Had we had to cycle along roads our parents would never have let us do it, but the canal had a good path and was car-free almost to the school gates. Even better, the first part of it was on Dad's cycle to work – we'd set off together, hammer it downhill and then, when we reached the canal, he would go left and we would go right.

JONNY

It was always a rush. Alistair never wanted to wait for me, and I never wanted to lose him. One time he had to get to school for an exam. He got a puncture and he just pushed his bike at me, grabbed mine, threw the repair kit over his shoulder and said, 'Fix it!' I'd never repaired a puncture in my life. I had to dip the inner tube in the canal to check where the puncture was, but I had to break the ice on the water first. It taught me how to fix a puncture but I almost froze to death. And I was very, very late for school.

We learned quickly how to make the ride as fast as possible. Little brother Ed used to go on the bus, so we'd make him carry our bags or take our blazers. If it rained you'd turn up with your clothes soaking, but it was quicker than taking the bus, and it allowed you to do it in your own time.

ALISTAIR

I should point out that we also worked as a team in Jonny's favour. On one occasion when his bike got a puncture, I gave him a backie on mine while he leaned out and pushed the other one along beside us.

When we actually got off our bikes at the gates, we walked into a school with a sporting culture that couldn't have been more conducive to our development. The key teacher for us at Bradford Grammar was Tony Kingham. He had been there since 1968, and ran the cross-country team. Among the runners he had guided was Richard Nerurkar, who went on to run for Britain at two Olympics.

He first noticed my running at junior school, and he still talks about a school relay I did then, as the last man in a team of four, each running 4 kilometres; I set off about 80 metres down and managed to come through to win it. I asked him recently whether, watching us run as young teenagers, he had any inkling what level we might end up at. He told me he'd noticed that, whenever we were presented with a new challenge, we managed to step up.

Mr Kingham was responsible for the running culture that allowed us to leave the premises at lunchtime and disappear off by ourselves for runs. We would go out every day. On Tuesday we might do a time trial; on Wednesday, an afternoon that was left free for sport, we might do a long run. But the teachers gave us complete freedom to do what we wanted. Mr Kingham's attitude was that you had to trust older lads. And nothing ever went wrong, although I would be so tired after some of the time trials in Lister Park that I would be struggling to stay awake in the afternoon lessons.

There were races most Saturdays during the winter and, if not, Mr Kingham would organize one – a relay, or a run through the woods. Most weeks we'd have fifty of us out. Jonny and I would never dream of missing those sessions. We were also running for Bingley Harriers, but I'm sure we wouldn't have got into running anywhere near as much without the school's unique attitude. At one point all three of us Brownlee brothers were Bradford Schools AA cross-country champions – me at under-sixteen, Jonny at under-fourteen and Ed aged nine. We must have been doing something right.

Being allowed to disappear for runs at lunchtime was wonderful. You would get changed at the very start of your lunch break and then off you went. You could, in effect, leave school, and that's exciting when you're eleven. From that point on I associated running with freedom; I would stare out of the window during morning lessons, thinking about where I might run that day.

I abused it a bit. I'd get fish and chips every Friday, or go to the bakery on the way back. There's an area in the middle of Bradford called Heaton Woods where we would often do Mr Kingham's organized runs. Well, we would run there all right, but then the messing around would begin. Because the woods were a bit dodgy, you'd find lots of half-burned car tyres dumped there. We would push them up to the top of a hill and roll them down, see how far we could get them to bounce.

JONNY

There would be certain regular running loops around Bradford, and everyone would know the best times they'd ever been run. Oh, Richard Nerurkar ran this time at Lister Park, another guy did that.

The school running club was also an actual registered running club, so you could compete for them in club competitions. I raced all my races – Northern Champs, National Champs – for the school. The best bit about going running at lunchtime? You were allowed to go to the front of the lunch queue. Priceless.

ALISTAIR

By the time I was in the sixth form the teachers didn't seem to care if I was going to any registrations – if I was running, I was running. It didn't matter. As long as I didn't miss any lessons and I was doing my schoolwork they were fine about it.

We were even fortunate with the school's attitude to swimming. At one point our early morning training was becoming a struggle: our regular pool was in the centre of Leeds, so we would have to absolutely nail it across town to the train station and then get lucky with the fast train from Leeds to Bradford station, which was about a kilometre from our school, then we'd have to run as fast as we could to make it into the classroom on time. By chance, City of Bradford trained in the school's pool after lessons. Shortly after we joined the club the school knocked down the old building and built that fantastic new pool. It all fell into place for us.

I was in Mr Kingham's form for two years. He also taught me French, and he knew very well that I'd rattle through my homework so I could go out on my bike. I think he finds it rather surreal watching us on television as we compete, but he's still a fantastic supporter; he was on board one of the two coaches laid on by Bingley Harriers to take people down from Yorkshire to watch us at the London Olympics.

JONNY

Of the eccentrics and obsessives, Dave Woodhead stood out by a mile. He and his wife, Eileen, have been organizing their series of fell races on the Bronte moors above Haworth, not far from their home in Keighley, for about quarter of a century. Their enthusiasm and attitude is infamous, if not borderline insane.

Everything has to be fun. Everything has to be hard. Their attitude to endurance sport informed ours as kids and has stuck with us ever since: you have to enjoy it. If you don't enjoy it, what's the point?

There were five groups of races spread over the year – the 12 kilometre Stanbury Splash in January, the 3 mile Bunny Runs over Easter, Skyline and the Stoop later in the year and the brilliant Auld Lang Syne race, just under 10 kilometres, on New Year's Eve. We did them as kids and we still do them now if we can. Dave's that kind of bloke. He draws you in and you can't say no. He may actually be the most enthusiastic man in the whole world.

ALISTAIR

I did my first Bunny Run in 2000, talked into it by a schoolmate at Bradford Grammar named Nick Howard. I was eleven years old and we formed a new club on the spot: name, Yorkshire

Youngsters; total membership, two. If it wasn't a particularly auspicious beginning – I finished 57th out of 228 – it was the start of a long and fruitful partnership.

A year later I was winning my first Dave race. It was the year of the foot-and-mouth outbreak, and the big Stoop race, doubling up as the Yorkshire Fell Running Championships, was switched to the Sunday before Christmas. When I was handed my race number perhaps I should have seen it as an omen: it was number one. Thankfully, I came home alone and out front.

Since then those fell races have become part of our racing lives. The Bunny Runs incorporate separate 'egg stages', with your reward being an enormous amount of chocolate – a very Dave prize.

By the time I'd reached the under-sixteens I'd won nine of these stages, and in 2005 I even decided to form my own relay team of one, called – quite appropriately – Mr No Friends. I finished fifth, completely covered in stinking mud. There's a self-explanatory part of the course up top called the Bog Monster, and I'd fallen straight in. An old chap was filming it all on his video camera, probably hoping that someone would do exactly what I had done. I think I rather shocked him with my language – 'the rudest words I've ever heard coming from a seventeen-year-old's mouth' – was how he put it to Dave. What he didn't realize was that it wasn't the cold, smelly mud that had pissed me off. It was losing two places. I'd been third until that point.

However, there were serious undertones to all those races; as well as being a touch unhinged, Dave was the team manager for England fell-running, and he took careful note of every one of my Yorkshire titles as they piled up, from under-fourteen to under-twenty-three.

Dave always reminds us of a Bunny Run when the two of us

were running as a team. The baton was an actual egg; come home without it and you were disqualified. I was doing the last two legs, Jonny the first, and as we came to the all-important handover the egg somehow slipped between his fingers and smashed on the turf. I had no choice – I reached down, scooped up the mess of shell, yolk and white and set off, eggshell spraying everywhere. Dave still has a photo of the moment. He used it as the background for his Bunny Run race numbers in Olympic year – these two skinny kids, horror all over their faces, frozen in black and white panic for all time.

It wasn't the glamour end of the sport. You began at an exposed gravel car park on top of a bleak moor, surrounded by small disused quarries. Dave always claimed the pavilion where you registered for races was the highest cricket club in England, in which case I hope the players all brought two jumpers and were allowed to wear woolly hats. The course took you twisting in and out of the quarries, always heading up and down, never flat, but often very fast when gravity was on your side.

Dave could embarrass you, especially if you were a shy teenager. In a race of his at Keswick in 2005 the winning athletes had to be photographed leaning on a replica of Penelope Pitstop's pink Cadillac. I have no idea where he got it from, and I have no idea why he insisted on us all wearing matching pink deely-boppers, but he did. I desperately wanted to avoid it, and I couldn't.

The Bunnys coincide with our birthdays. Sure enough, Dave has always secretly arranged for us to be stuck on the top table in the pub afterwards, in front of hundreds of people, and be serenaded with 'Happy Birthday'. I'm as embarrassed by it now as I was aged twelve.

The only race of his that neither of us has won is one of those Bunny Runs. We've done the rest, but the closest we've come in a Bunny is second – Jonny in 2008, me in 2006, when I was beaten by three seconds by a bloke called Mark Buckingham. It isn't over, though, not by a long way. It's not about the prizes; the best I got for winning Auld Lang Syne was a balloon-making kit, and I was so exhausted I didn't have enough breath left to blow up a sausage dog. It's about pride. I have a £50 bet with Dave that I will win one. I've got until 2014; believe me when I say that nothing – nothing – will stop me.

Dave told me recently, in one of his reflective moments, that of the two of us he always thought Jonny had the more talent. The rationale was simple: Jonny was quieter, he took more in. He thought of me as smarter, but at the same time able to get away with things – like the time I set up a card school at one of the fell-running training camps, using chocolate raisins in lieu of coins, and then, when we were about to get in trouble for it, managing to ditch my stash so that I came out of it as the innocent party.

There must have been signs, to someone as shrewd as Dave, that the pair of us had something. He still has a copy of a magazine he edited called *The Fell Runner*, featuring a little article I wrote at the age of twelve. The subject: 'I want to race at an Olympics'. It upsets him that he failed to put money on me fulfilling my dream.

JONNY

Our most formative swimming coach when we were young had the unlikely name of Corinne Tantrum, or Coz to those under her tutelage.

We had begun training at Aireborough leisure centre, Guiseley, in November 1995. Alistair was seven, I was five. We first worked under a coach we called Shouty John, who unsurprisingly scared me rigid. The pool had its own unique feel: a cold-water foot-well as you came out of the changing rooms, a ridiculously cavernous deep end and a strange length – 27.5 yards, a few inches too long to be any good for timings. In its favour was a little tuck shop they used to open up on club night.

From there we were spotted and taken into the system at the prestigious City of Leeds club. The set-up couldn't have been more contrasting. Leeds International Pool was a huge, overwhelming place with deep murky waters, enormous diving pits and an aura of accomplishment and gravitas. It was there that we met Andy Pearce, a coach who played another key role in our development. Andy was something of a local legend, the holder of several long-distance swimming records and a fine coach who managed to keep the sessions strong but fun. He would take me, aged nine, to my first Yorkshire Championships, where I would win the 50 metre backstroke title. Six years on, when he moved from Leeds to City of Bradford, he would again coach me with distinction.

Leeds had a reputation as a production line of talent. Olympic medallists Adrian Moorhouse and James Hickman had both come through, and the system was built around pure swimming: eight two-hour sessions a week. Alistair and I were both county-level swimmers, but more than that we were triathletes. Eight sessions was too much for us, but when we asked if we could do fewer, to leave room for our cycling and running, we were told it was all or nothing.

Nothing it was. Corinne got the call at City of Bradford, where she coached six sessions a week. Mum and Dad were concerned that the same thing was going to happen again, that we would be turfed out if she discovered we were actually triathletes. We were under strict instructions not to tell anyone our big secret. So we were rather shocked when, as we walked out on to the poolside for the first time, she announced, 'Here they are, our new triathletes!'

That's Coz. Entirely no-nonsense. It worked perfectly for us. She coached swimming for some of the monthly northern tri camps, so she understood our lean towards open-water swimming, and realized that we needed to focus more on things like 400-metre sets rather than sprints.

She describes us as chalk and cheese. Alistair always turned up fresh from a run, covered in mud and dripping wet, having to be sent back to the showers to get cleaned up before he was allowed in the water. In those days, remarkably, he was always early – poolside at least fifteen minutes before the session started, helping to put out the lane ropes. Me? I was outside playing football, always the last one ready, usually missing the first 100 metres because I was chatting to Coz, doing anything I could to delay getting in.

Coz says I would float through sessions if she let me. She had to get under my skin, into my ear, to get anything out of me. I would be messing about, chatting to everyone, pulling the legs of the swimmers in front for a laugh. Alistair, if she told him she wanted two lengths done in 35 seconds, would make sure he hit it in exactly 34. Not just what was asked, but proving he could do better.

She remembers me following Al around like a lapdog. I prefer her memories of what we were like with the girls. Apparently I was able to talk to them very easily, and they thought I was 'the bee's knees' – her words, not mine. Al? They thought he was a bit weird.

Our routine was soon established. On Mondays and late on Fridays we would swim at Shipley, on Tuesdays and Sundays at Rhodesway Pool, and on Thursdays at our school pool at Bradford Grammar, which had something of a Hogwarts feel – Roman bath-style pillars, tiny tiles like a mosaic, the place looking like it hadn't been redecorated since the Middle Ages. Eventually they closed it down, probably donating the old bricks to a museum, and installed a pristine new pool: beautifully clean, airy and light, a complete contrast.

Coz once asked Alistair to train according to certain heart-rate zones – 200 metres at 120 beats per minute, 200 metres at 100 bpm. It's a way of knowing exactly how hard you are pushing yourself. He came back the next week with the print-outs he'd made and showed her, with great pride, how he had hit each target absolutely spot on. She still has them now.

When Alistair was fourteen and I was twelve, Coz took a call from Jack Maitland, British Triathlon's local coach and the man who still helps guide us. The BTF were said to be unhappy with the amount of swimming we were doing. They thought the balance with running and cycling was wrong, and that the volume was too high for lads of our age. The idea was that we would listen to Coz when we might not listen to others. She spoke to Dad, and then she spoke to Alistair. He listened, but he was quite firm: 'I want to be an Olympic champion. I will be an Olympic champion. I know what I can cope with. If I want to be a champion in ten years' time, I have to be doing what they'll be doing in ten years' time. I know what I'm doing.'

ALISTAIR

That was the running and swimming taken care of. Our cycling education came courtesy of a little tri shop in Horsforth called Triangle, and a man called Adam Nevins who ran the place.

It wasn't big – just a little corner shop, crammed with bikes and little gems of cycling memorabilia. But this was at a time when there were almost no triathlon shops anywhere in the country, and here we were with one half a mile down the road from our parents' house. On such little details do lives change.

Adam seemed so tall and imposing on that first visit, almost intimidatingly knowledgeable, but he was brilliant with us. We were just skinny kids who were into triathlon, but he took us into the inner circle and weekend after weekend he taught us the intricacies and secrets of road riding and the Yorkshire scene.

He had started up a racing team at the shop, but he would let the local lads join the team on the long Sunday club rides when he felt they were old enough to cope. In his youth Adam had learned his trade with Bradford Wheelers, which, with Manchester Wheelers, were the two big clubs. He had been initiated by his elders, and he did the same with us: a lecture every time we went into Triangle, lessons in group riding out on the roads, a new route every weekend.

Every time we went in there – and as lads obsessed with cycling and triathlon we went in there a lot – Adam would dish out advice: try a bit of turbo-training, lads; don't eat anything too sugary before your rides or you'll have a sugar high and then a sugar low; when it's raining, lads, there's no point riding your bike because your legs get too cold. He gave Jonny his first bike top, which he wore until it fell apart, and he introduced us to other young riders who would become key training partners in the years ahead.

More importantly than anything else, Adam taught us how to ride in a group, and the secret cycling routes across Yorkshire that only the insiders and veterans know. I remember doing some hellishly long rides with him. We both certainly did our first 100 mile rides with the Triangle group. Jonny was barely old enough to handle it, even with the obligatory café stop for teacakes halfway round – on one of the early long ones, when we cycled way out into Lancashire and the Forest of Boland, he managed to get back as far as Skipton, still 20-odd miles from home, and was so tired he just rolled to a stop by a phone box and called Dad to ask for a lift home. He spent his last few quid buying as much as he could in the local bakery, and then sat on the pavement, all on his own, to eat his pasties and wait for Dad to arrive.

We would simply listen and learn, and whatever Adam told us one week we would make sure we were doing the week after. A lot of coaching is about passing certain levels and achieving grades. Adam's was the antithesis of that. It was all about fun, all about adventure. 'Right, let's race to the next lamp post.' 'Let's have a café stop up there.' We would lean the bikes against a wall, letting the rest of the group watch them while they had coffee and cake, and nip off to grab a bag of sweets or race another little loop.

JONNY

My first proper, brand-new racing bike came from Adam at Triangle. I'd started off on an old second-hand Peugeot, Al on a Raleigh Flyer. Both were old-school: brakes on the top bars, gears on the downtube. Then it was just hand-me-downs from Alistair, including an old Giant racer and Giant mountain bike that made me feel like a professional sponsored athlete because my branding was ubiquitous.

The Triangle one was the best Christmas present I'll ever get. I sprinted downstairs on Christmas morning and spotted a racing bike. But Alistair was looking for a bike at the same time. Aargh, I thought, that must be Alistair's. Then I looked at the label and saw it was mine. Oh, the surprise, the delight.

I could not wait to get out on it. Predictably it then snowed for the next week. I couldn't go out on the damn thing for days. I looked at it lovingly every morning, stroked it, polished it.

I rode that bike to death. Even years later, when I was racing and trying to qualify for Great Britain, I was on the same ridiculously small bike, with the saddle up as high as it could go. This was the time when they thought small wheels were good for triathlon, so I was riding with 650 centimetre wheels. Dad told me the small wheels were good for cornering, and who disagrees with their dad when they're a kid? When I did make the step up to the GB programme I was handed a top-of-the-range, all-carbon Trek bike. The first time I rode that I could barely believe how light and fast it was.

ALISTAIR

Our first real triathlon bikes were both Triangle specials. Adam bought in some tri-specific frames, had them decalled up in the shop livery and built them up with Campagnolo components. We loved them, but then again, he could have given us a brace of penny farthings and we would have ridden them. We rode those bikes to bits, and Adam was the one who had to pick up the pieces, often quite literally. We would take them into the shop with the wheels falling apart and gear mech bunged up with mud and rust. But what's a bike for if not to be ridden hard?

The new Triangle shop is far grander than the original. There's much more space, a workshop down in the cellar that smells of oil but is as organized as a laboratory, Italian cycling references everywhere and a set of our swim-hats displayed on the wall. But it is still Triangle. There are no barcode scanners or high-tech tills, just handwritten price tags and old manual tills.

Speak to Adam now and he'll tell you that he always felt a bit sorry for Jonny, who got the hand-me-down bikes and kit, and seemed almost in awe of his big brother. But he and the older guys always thought Jonny would ultimately become the better athlete, because of his attitude. We would both listen to the advice we were being given, but Jonny would really think about it, analyse the hell out of it.

JONNY

We loved those long weekend rides. The British Triathlon belief was that we should be doing only short stuff. The Adam Nevins belief was: 'Screw that.' We'd go 95 miles, 100 miles, into the Dales, into the hills.

These were the rides that shaped us as cyclists. Adam's wife came out with us one time, and she was struggling a little. Alistair rode alongside her, encouraging her. He turned the reduced pace to his advantage by balancing his revision notes for his physics A-Level on the handlebars and reading intently as he pedalled along.

Two of the great things about cycling in Yorkshire are the culture around it and the informal tribe of old boys who formed it. There're ones who know every hole in the road. Every pothole. It's awesome. You'd go out for a ride in those days and see loads of them, and we still do.

Our mate Nathan's granddad Alan – known as 'Young Alan' in Yorkshire cycling circles – is a great case in point. Even now he's still organizing races. You see him out almost every day on his tandem with his wife.

Alan and the old boys will ride out every Saturday morning from the Leeds ring road at Lawnswood to Bolton Abbey up the Wharfe Valley and back. We would head out with them, aged twelve compared to their sixty and seventy, to shouts of, 'You all right, youngster?' We'd head to a rural café, have toasted tea-cakes and ride back. As we got better we'd ride out with them and stick on an extra loop before the finish. Get there, nail the extra miles really quickly, get back before they're ready to leave the café.

With Young Alan was an old chap named Tony, who was always the live wire. Halfway through the ride he'd give you a look and say, 'Come on, youngster, let's attack . . .' And you'd attack off the front of the group, all the rest of them protesting, 'Ooh, it's an easy ride, this . . .' He'd shout at you, 'Ignore the old gits!' – and he was the oldest one there. 'Come on, we're just having a bit of fun!'

All of them all still follow what we do now. We never knew they cared. Tony turned up at our house one day in Olympic year. 'Lads, I've been watching on TV.' He'd seen the house on a documentary we had done, recognized where it was and thought he'd pop in for a visit. He comes quite regularly now, and always leaves his wife sitting in the car outside. We ask him if he wants to come in for a cup of tea. 'No, wife's in car.' He'll stand there for twenty minutes. 'I don't want to keep you lads, but . . .'

The final key character in those early days was Jack Maitland, the man who still shares our coaching.

Back then Jack was in charge of the northern training camps, one of the regional get-togethers run by British Triathlon for developing athletes. One weekend every month throughout the winter the Yorkshire region would have a camp for everyone aged from fourteen to eighteen, and it was absolutely brilliant. We would have a weekend at the Manchester Velodrome, another swimming at Ponds Forge in Sheffield, another in the Dales, where we'd hire a cottage and go mountain-biking.

Jack had spotted our results in children's races, and although he had to wait until we were old enough before asking us to those camps, he says now that we were both very independent for lads of that age. When you were invited along the instructions said you could either be driven there or you could be picked up from the nearest train station. I think Alistair was the first one who ever took the second option.

Jack has a theory that has been borne out in us, which is that you need to love what you are doing if you are going to develop into a successful senior athlete. Others will drop away if they're being pushed into it by parents. To make it you have to love training more than anything else, and in particular you have to love the bike.

He first noticed that Alistair might have something special on a national camp in Market Bosworth. They were doing a swim set designed to practise their entry and exit, and Jack was standing out in the water as the first buoy. He decided to make it competitive by running a 'devil take the hindmost' format on each lap, where the last lad through each time would drop out. At the time Al was one of the youngest in the group, and definitely one of the smallest. But Jack remembers him hammering it towards the suicidal inside route every time to make sure he was never last, even if it meant that he took a terrible battering from the bigger lads. He kept doing it, and it kept working. That was the point when he said to himself, 'Wow, that's someone who'll go on to make it.'

When I started going on those camps I was fourteen and Alistair sixteen. He was allowed to ride with the big lads, the fast ones who were two years older than he was. I was left with the younger ones. It was a big motivation for me, because I wanted to ride with him. I wanted to be thought of as one of the big boys.

ALISTAIR

Jack has told me that Jonny stood out for his maturity. When he was fifteen he was racing at Eton in a qualifier for the European Youth Relays; to get picked for the Great Britain team for the first time you had to impress in that single race. Jonny jumped on his bike and – crack! His seat-post snapped. That was it – his big dream was over. Naturally he was devastated, but what made Jack take note was that he recovered from that disappointment very quickly. He proved that he could overcome obstacles, rather than being floored by them.

Those northern camps were both brutal and an enormous amount of fun. On one of them we had to run up Ingleborough, the second highest peak in the Yorkshire Dales. As we left the youth hostel where we were staying, all of us in running vests and shorts, the snow started to come in horizontally. With every 50 metres climbed the snow got heavier and the wind stronger. Tops and tights kept coming out of our backpacks, but the temperature was dropping faster than we could warm up. By the time we reached the top we were forced to take shelter behind a little stone wall, the entire summit a deserted white-out, not even a rock visible, with none of us having any idea where the edge was. Jack was all smiles. 'Don't worry, I've taken a compass bearing, we'll be fine.'

We might have been, but it was so windy you couldn't hear anything he was saying. We just had to run for it as a group. And as we ran down the other side, we saw the only other people we would see on the peak all day – all of them wearing crampons, carrying ice axes and all tied together. They looked as surprised at the sight of us as they would have been at the sight of zebras.

On another camp, in Ingleton, when we'd been training hard

all day, they told us they had a special treat lined up for us in the evening. It turned out to be taking us down the caves and into the potholes. We were fine about it; the guy visiting us from British Triathlon less so. He was a sleek southerner on a tour of all the various regional camps, and he couldn't stop moaning: 'Trust my luck, I visit the northern camp and I have to go down a bloody hole!'

Faced with those sorts of adventures, the kids who were always going to drop out did drop out. The two of us would have wanted to do all that good stuff anyway, but the motivating factor of having those camps every single month all the way through every winter, learning from people who were older than you, was critical to our development.

JONNY

A lot of people found it too hard. British Triathlon once had a national camp at one of our northern bases. It was a bunk cabin. All hell broke loose – people saying, 'I'm not running on that moor, it's too cold.' Everyone else would be looking for training venues with a nice pool and good bike routes, and Jack would say, 'Don't worry about swimming this time, we'll just go to this bunk cabin; we'll just ride and run.' That taught us to adapt our training. When it was too snowy to go out on the roads, we'd go mountain-biking instead.

We'll still do it now. Last winter I was out mountain-biking on the moors and I fell through a load of ice into a frozen pond. It was horrible, but I still rode back. I was so cold I couldn't even open the front door. I had to jump into my bed with all my clothes on. It felt like I was back on one of those northern camps. Half-frozen, but on a fantastic adventure.

Climbing the Summit

ALISTAIR

I was eleven when I first decided I would train with a target in mind. It was the end of the Christmas term in 2000, and a friend of mine was showing off his Yorkshire representative running vest, which was making me feel rather jealous. He noticed this, and told me that if you came in the top eight in the County Championships in January then you automatically got both a vest and the chance to run for the county. I thought that was absolutely amazing. There were three weeks over the Christmas holidays before the championships and I thought: right, I'm going to train really bloody hard.

Up to that point it had all been coming from the outside – your parents take you to swimming, or you go running with them. This was the first time I thought: I'm going to take control of this.

It worked. In the race at Rotherham I finished seventh, got in the team and got my Yorkshire vest. But I soon realized that didn't feel enough. I decided I wanted to win it.

The following year's championships were being held at Bodington Hall, just off the Otley Road in the northern outskirts of Leeds, which is where I now train every Saturday. Once again, I trained really hard over the Christmas holidays – going off on runs on my own, pushing myself, thinking how much I wanted to come out on top.

Sure enough, the hard work paid dividends. It felt like I won by miles; although it was probably only about 50 metres, I suppose that is quite a margin when the entire race is only 3 kilometres. I can remember both the medal and the reception. One came in a little box, and still lives in my treasure chest of trophies at the family home. The other featured Mum, Dad and Granddad. I was covered in mud, freezing cold, shivering. Granddad took one look at me, took off his coat and draped it round my shoulders.

I've always hated the word 'goal'. Whenever a coach has told me to set goals, I think: who cares, I just want to go out training. But I guess I'd set myself a goal back then without consciously realizing it. I knew I wanted to win the Yorkshire Championships, and then went away to train for it. Winning felt wonderful.

Even then, however, I was aware that it was a step rather than the final destination. Those early cross-country races were the first time I became aware of what motivation could do for you. Even running in the West Yorkshire leagues I'd know I wanted to win those races and win them easily. Then you would move on to the next stage up, the North of England Championships, where I came second time and time again. I remember thinking that this was the best quality race I could win – the Inter-Counties and the Nationals seemed too far off – but the ambition had been unleashed. I was always looking above myself, trying to do better; I was never happy enough winning the local race or the regional race.

Every year the rivalries would be different. I was doing cross-country, fell races, triathlon, and you would come up against different competitors wherever you went. Adam Hickey was the toughest one in running. He was a phenomenal cross-country runner, far better than me – he used to win everything all the way up to the age of sixteen, by enormous margins, and he could swim on top of that, so he could beat me in triathlons too. He was a big kid, so much stronger than me, and had so much natural talent. There was a whole group of them who came out of Southend. The Essex boys. They swept the board; one year at the Nationals they took the first four places.

By the age of fourteen I was ready to have a crack at winning my first Great Britain vest by trying to qualify for the team for the European Youth Relays. I knew Adam would qualify, but with three lads per team I knew I had a chance, even though I was the youngest in my two-year age category.

The qualifying race was held at Rivington Pike, a reservoir a few miles north-west of Bolton. It was old-school – jump in a freezing lake, run miles to transition, a glamour-free environment – and I was also less than fresh. Earlier in the day, I had run the qualifiers for the England fell-running team. But I managed to finish in the top three, and that was me off to Graz in Austria for my first experience of international competition, of being handed GB kit.

When you're fourteen that kit blows you away, even though in hindsight the stuff was a horror show. Those were the days – very dark days – when you did triathlon in skimpy Speedos and a crop top. I was so small and skinny that even the smallest vest, which was supposedly skin-tight, was hanging off me. I tried telling them I couldn't swim in it. It was like towing a parachute. They advised me to roll the vest down, stick it in my trunks, swim with it down there and then whip it out when I came out of the water.

I went on the first leg, with Gavin Stokes on second and Adam Hickey on the anchor. Even as I lined up for the 200 metre swim, 5 kilometre bike and 2.5 kilometre run one of the officials didn't want to let me race – I was so small that he was convinced I couldn't possibly be old enough. Admittedly I was a full year younger than everyone else (I was fourteen, everyone else was fifteen) but even then I was tiny. And we won the thing. I was starting to develop a taste for it.

I was also about to start appreciating how good it felt to be fit and in form. When I qualified for the Youth Relays again the following year, and this time went to Hungary, it was as painful an experience as Graz had been glorious. Little did I know it as I set off on the run leg of the race, but I already had a stress fracture. I went off hard, as I always liked to do, and as we went over a section of cobblestones I just heard my foot go CRACK!

I had two more kilometres to run, with a fractured foot, but to me that wasn't an excuse – I still had to finish, because mine was the first leg of the team relay. Yet if the theory behind that was exemplary, the reality was more chastening. I was last by miles, and in so much pain coming towards the finish on the waterfront that I fainted and fell off a jetty. I hit the water, had to swim to a ladder, climb all the way back up and start running again.

My progression as a young athlete continued to be anything but linear. Even though I qualified for the World Junior Championships in Japan in 2005, I was dreadful when I got there. It was all a huge shock to me, from the travel to the racing. As a kid from Leeds I had no idea about how strange Japan would feel, and not much more about how hot it would be. As far as the racing went, I had gone to Japan as the second-best young triathlete in Britain, yet on a global level I was absolutely nowhere. I was dreadful at the European Juniors that year too. I simply wasn't prepared for how big the step up in class would be. Admittedly I was two years younger than almost everyone else in the field, but I just wasn't close; Olly Freeman, the leading Briton, was miles better than me.

But, if anything, that year between 2005 and 2006 was indispensable. It worked as a massive kick up the arse. I vowed that I'd never again go to a race simply having qualified. That would no longer be enough. If I was going to go, I wanted to go to win. I was almost disgusted with myself that I'd thought qualifying was an impressive thing. I came back and my coach Malcolm Brown had been going through exactly the same thought process. 'You must never go to the other side of the world to race that badly again.'

I improved more in that period than at any other time before or since. The first benchmark for that was finally winning the English Schools Cross Country Championships after years of trying and failing – ninth, eleventh, tenth . . . No matter that they were going on at the same time as the World Championships, meaning that runners who had qualified for that weren't there. My friends remind me to this day that I should always be known as the bloke who won the championships when the best were elsewhere, but I quietened them down by then coming in fourth at the junior men's National Cross Country Championships.

I'd been very beatable before then. I had good races, but I'd never been consistently good, let alone in a class of my own, but the new attitude and long hours of hard work were starting to yield dividends. At school I had more time to go running between lessons. I was cycling to school most days, and I'd found a swimming routine which allowed me to train hard and regularly. Physical maturity must have come into it too. I was quite late in going through puberty, quite late in starting to get close to my adult size, but finally it was happening.

By this stage I knew that I wanted to be an athlete. In a careers session the teacher came round the classroom, being very grammar school about it all: 'What do *you* want to be, boy?' The answers kept coming: brain surgeon, commercial lawyer, until my turn came, and I gave my unusual answer: I want to be a professional athlete. The teacher looked at me and frowned. 'Is that actually possible, boy?'

I can't be too hard on him. Even if he had heard of triathlon, I'm not sure he had any idea what my racing background was. A few minutes later, he said: 'Well, boys, you've got it right. It doesn't matter what you do. You'll never do a day's work in your life if you enjoy what you're doing for a living.'

There was one problem: I wasn't at all sure if being a professional triathlete was actually possible. There was no clearly defined career path as there is in other sports, no academy like league football clubs have, no trainee schemes. That's why I applied to go to university, even though I was equally aware that I wasn't doing it properly and had no real desire to go. Other people applying to do medicine were doing extra homework sessions, or practice interviews, but I never bothered.

I applied to four places, including Girton College at Cambridge. Our essay question in the entrance exam was: 'A little knowledge can be a dangerous thing. Discuss.' All I could think about was getting back to Leeds to do a bike ride. When I opened a letter one morning that told me I had been accepted, I was as surprised as my teachers. The headmaster came up to me later that day and looked at me quizzically. 'So, Alistair. Are you actually going to go?'

I had other priorities. Straight after one of my A-Levels I flew to the European Championships in Autun, turning up so late I didn't even have a chance to look at the course. I raced the next morning and came third behind France's Aurélien Raphaël and Russia's Alexander Bryukhankov. While the overall result was disappointing – I'd swum badly and biked only okay – I took small comfort in the fact that I had run a minute faster than everyone else. And I'd run a faster 5 kilometres in my race than the seniors did as part of their 10 kilometres, so that kept my mood up.

By that stage I was starting to get noticed. But I thought, this is only the Europeans; the Worlds are where it really is. I was very aware that the Europeans were only a stepping stone.

The performance director of British Triathlon gave us a big speech after those under-twenty-three championships. The men had got medals in all age groups, and he told us how that was fantastic, but that the Worlds were in six weeks, and we shouldn't lose focus. I sat there thinking: 'That's obvious.'

I wanted to go away and train really hard. The trouble was, it was the middle of summer, and everything had shut down. The swimming clubs were closed; the running sessions had finished. So I started training with local lads, swimming at seven thirty every morning.

The Worlds were in Lausanne. I was aware that although I wasn't the favourite, I still had a chance of winning it. And I really wanted to win it. Jonny had qualified for it too. I was a year underage, but he was three years under. Bloody hell, I thought, if Jonny gets a lucky swim and nips ahead of me, how annoying will that be?

I went through the field beforehand to try to pick out the real danger men. One in particular stood out: a guy from the USA called Steven Duplinksy. I knew he was a faster runner than me, so I told the coaches, 'I don't care about anyone else in the field – just tell me where Duplinsky is.' I passed the first coach on the bike leg and looked up for the news. 'He's nowhere, Alistair! Minute forty down!' It hit me: I've won this . . .

Even now it's difficult to recall the details of those races accurately. When I was winning, did I cruise them? When you win, and you win well, you cut out a lot of the nasty bits en route. The dominant memory is of the victory. But after winning those

World Juniors I remember telling someone that I didn't feel I'd run that well, because it had felt hard. And they told me that big wins should usually feel hard, because then you know you've got the most out of yourself – you've pushed as much as you can.

At no point in my development did I ever think: I can't do this, I shouldn't be here. It all felt entirely natural.

A big win changes everything. It opens so many doors. You are catapulted up levels in funding programmes. Sponsors suddenly notice you. You are approached by agents, who talk to you about a career as a professional athlete.

Winning the World Juniors really was a big thing for me. It was as though a switch clicked in my head. I knew that every world junior champion had gone on to have a good senior career. And the progression came rapidly after Lausanne. I was introduced to Richard Downey, the agent I am still with; I was signed by some sponsors; I was awarded £5,000 a year Lottery funding. Suddenly becoming a triathlete full-time was a genuine possibility, even though my place at Cambridge was still open to me.

That pivotal decision was still to come. I had already made my senior bow with the big boys, at the British Championships being held within the Royal Windsor Triathlon. There was a prize of £1,500 for the winner, which seemed like an awful lot of money to a young kid from Yorkshire, so my mate Phil Graves and I hatched a plan to see if we could snatch it from under the favourites' noses. It was hardly the most complicated strategy: we were going to get ourselves up into the main pack on the bike and attack off the front. I was convinced that if we could get a lead of two minutes then that would be it – I'd have the race in the bag. Phil could have half my £1,500 for his hard work on the swim and bike.

We get halfway round the bike leg and – bang! We go for it. It looks like it's worked – there's me, Phil and Marc Jenkins off the front. No one has the faintest idea who Phil and I are, so they don't really care about chasing us down. It's also the hottest day Windsor's ever known, so everyone is suffering. I'm doing my best to work it hard at the front, shouting at Phil to come through and do his turn. He's in bits. 'I can't, mate. I'm screwed.'

We get to the outskirts of Windsor. It isn't a big place. But it takes ages to get back to transition. Roundabout after roundabout, all the way round the houses and back again, and the legs were on fire. The run starts, Jenkins goes away, and then suddenly I'm overtaking him. I can't believe it. I'm winning the Nationals. This is amazing! I'm feeling wonderful!

At 7 kilometres it went dramatically wrong. From coasting I juddered to the most almighty halt, which made sense: it was only the second Olympic distance race I'd ever done. In the space of a few hundred metres I went from first to twelfth. They all came past me. But I had made an impact, and I had shown myself what I might be able to do.

JONNY

My own competitive career began when I was aged nine, with my first swimming gala. It was at Aireborough pool where we used to have our lessons.

I ended up with a few medals, which delighted me at the time even though it really was no big deal. I think I still hold a record going back to those days – the under-nine backstroke. I clocked about 19 seconds for the 25 metre course. The world hardly quaked, but those medals were the first I had ever won, and they meant something special to me. It was the start of a lifelong hunt for trophies.

In my last year at junior school came my first success out of the water, when I won something called the HMC cross-country. Think of it as a posh schools' showdown. This edition was held up at Giggleswick School. I was very conscious that Alistair had never won it. The best he ever managed was second. But I went out and won it, which absolutely delighted me.

It was the first biggish race in which I'd ever done really well, and I rather liked the feeling. Wow – I can win these things. To my young mind, because there were a lot of people there, it really meant something. So too did the way I won it. The organizers used to send out what they called a hare – an older boy who would lead the way, showing you the course so you didn't get lost. Well, we were going so fast that the hare couldn't handle the pace and had to drop out. Wow a second time – I can not only beat kids my own age, but I can beat a kid who's much older than me too.

The first time I actually trained for something was when I was trying to qualify for the Yorkshire Schools cross-country team, aged thirteen. It was Christmas, and I decided I would go for a run along the canal before we went to my uncle's house for the big lunch. He lived quite a long way away, so I had to be up early – but I did it, by myself, without anyone telling me to, or Alistair or my parents coming along with me. For the first time I didn't just turn up to a race and run; I prepared, and that too would become a lifelong habit.

So much of what turned out to be training was still pure fun. We would go out on our bikes with our mates at weekends for a laugh, head up to the Dales on camping trips, just messing around, finding new cafés, finding new places. We didn't go out on a boring straight road and think: we'll have to ride for two hours and turn round. We thought: we'll search for a café.

Alistair would always pretend he knew where to go. 'I've been here before. I know where I am.' He never did. As soon as he said that, the rest of us would look at each other. 'Oh no . . .'

There were times when we'd be walking across the fields with bikes on our shoulders. Alistair would be certain about it – 'There's a café near here, there's a café, there's one near Brimham Rocks.' One day, as was quite usual, the guys with us were really good cyclists, the best in their age groups, and we were all looking at each other, asking: where the hell is he taking us? Eventually we came across a path and some walkers. We asked about the café, to looks of confusion and disdain. 'There's never been a café round here.' Next week the same thing would happen all over again.

We loved being outside, and we could talk about a hill for ever. I remember arriving in the Lake District with the gang on one trip, and as usual we all decided to go for a ride. It was the depths of winter, only three p.m. but already dark. We didn't really know where we were going – round Coniston, on this tiny little road, lake on one side, woods on the other.

Suddenly I punctured. They were all telling me about the panthers that escaped and ran loose up there. I'm already pretty scared, then we hear this screaming in the woods. That was it – they all scarpered, leaving me there staring at my puncture.

You've never seen anyone pump up an inner tube so fast. Back on the bike, thrashing away at the pedals, expecting any moment to feel a panther's claws in my backside. At the first corner we came to, our friend Sam realized his brakes had failed too. Just as I caught up with the rest of the group the road bent sharp left, and Sam went straight on. 'See you later, lads!'

It was always all about the adventures, all about the fun. And we'd race each other, not for training but because it was fun.

There was a guy called Michael Kipling who I swam with at City of Leeds and then City of Bradford. He was at my school, same age; we won the National Schools Championships relay together. Every time I went swimming he was there, and I'm sure he inadvertently drove me on. It was the same everywhere I trained. At school there were all our running mates; for cycling we had the Triangle squad – we tapped into their network of riding partners and their knowledge of routes out into the lanes and Dales. Then there were the Edmondson brothers, Josh and Nathan, who are now making it as pro cyclists, Josh with Team Sky. I'm sure that we would never have done so much cycling, or realized how far you have to go, without those groups to push us. Before I met the Triangle group I thought a two-hour ride was a long way, but these guys would be going out for four hours. I'd never dreamed of that before; I wouldn't have known where to go even if I had.

In my third year at secondary school, when I was fourteen, I started turning some of that fun into results and took aim at getting into the English Schools cross-country team. I'd always been pretty good over the country from a young age, but then I had a period when I was convinced I was going to make it as a footballer for Leeds United and went away from the pure running side of things. At the trials I got an unpleasant surprise; a guy from my own school almost beat me. That had never happened before, and I didn't like it. My fitness from all those swimming lessons had always carried me through, but suddenly it was no longer enough. It hit me: what am I doing? I'm better than this. I'm better than this, but it won't happen unless I apply myself.

It was a huge turning point. For the first time, I really wanted it. I was ready to commit. On the way back from the race Dad and I stopped off at the big sports superstore Decathlon. A deal was struck: I told Dad I would ride every day if he bought me a new cycling top. And he did, and so did I.

I started training hard, and the results gradually came in. I won a place on British Triathlon's young athletes' programme, and qualified for my first overseas triathlon shortly afterwards, in the summer of that same year. It was in Belgium, and we drove over in a van – a taste of the foreign travel to come. With it came my first GB hoodie and my first GB jumper. I've still got them both. That also signalled the start of funding for me, with my very first chunk of money, which was another turning point.

The sight of Alistair, aged fourteen, bringing home his first Great Britain kit, after qualifying for the European Youth Relays, had been a pivotal moment. I saw his vest and was blown away – it's possible: someone from my family can be good enough to compete for our country. It was the same when he won the World Junior Championships. Until that point triathlon had been something that we did, not quite for fun, but not as a serious pursuit. It was a local scene involving only us and our friends. Suddenly Alistair was World Junior Champion, and the horizons expanded exponentially. We could actually do this on a world stage.

When it was my turn to qualify for the European Relays, in 2006, a few years after Alistair, and I went off to Rijeka in Croatia, that was the start of my own real journey into big-time international competition. I had the kit; I had the special pass that said 'ELITE ATHLETE' that allowed me to go wherever I wanted. I've kept all those passes to this day.

The format for the relays is simple: three of you in a team, each in turn doing a very short triathlon – 300 metre swim, 8 kilometre bike and 1.5 kilometre run. I took over from our mate Phil Graves for the third and final leg. At that point in my career I was a strong swimmer and runner and had a little bit of weakness on the bike, but Phil had handed over to me in good shape: I was in second, with Portugal's João Silva five seconds in front of me. The swim was almost surreal – all I could think about were all the fish I could see – and I'd closed in on him by the start of the run. Then, when we hit the big hill, that's when I went away and dropped him. As I ran away from him down that hill I remember the sensation of pride: I'm doing it, I'm winning a big race abroad.

They were holding the European Under-23 Championship at the same venue that weekend. I couldn't quite believe I was competing on the same course as Olly Freeman and Will Clarke. Nor could I believe it when I was woken up by them on the Saturday night, after their race but before mine the following day, as they came back from the pub in all sorts of bother. Will slept in a bush, at least for a while. He came into breakfast the next morning with leaves and straw all over his clothes.

At that point there was still no thought of the win being anything more than a great target and trophy in itself. I didn't see it as part of a linear adventure taking me to the Olympic podium. I was too young, and the gap seemed too great – not just to the senior men racing at the very top level, but to Olly and Will racing at under-twenty-three. I was very conscious that I was just a kid of sixteen.

Nor did anyone make much of a deal about it when I got home. It was the summer holiday, so there was no mention of it in school assembly as there was when you turned in a good cross-country result.

When I qualified for the World Junior Championships that same year the fuss was a little greater. I was still just sixteen, Alistair eighteen, and we were racing against guys aged all the way up to nineteen. It should have been beyond us, but it worked out brilliantly for one Brownlee brother – just not this one.

I had a great swim, coming out of the water five seconds clear of my brother. Then, going round the first big corner of the bike ride, around 5 kilometres in, I went down in a clattering crash, my tubular tyre rolling off as I hit the deck. I was a goner. I stumbled back to the start through all the traffic and crowds, crying my eyes out.

I got back to find out Alistair had won the whole thing. At the time that only made me even more pissed off. Then I heard that João Silva, the guy I'd beaten in the Youth Relays, had come third. It all seemed so unfair. I told Alistair that Silva's result meant I could have come third. He laughed that one out, telling me it was a completely different race.

How did I feel? I was gutted that he had no time for me. It was his first really big race win and, added to that, no British junior had won it for a long, long time, not since Tim Don. On that same weekend in Lausanne Will Clarke won the World Under-23 title and Tim won the World Championship. In all that, my little crash clearly interested no one.

We all went out for an ice cream afterwards – the whole family. I had no interest in going. I just wanted to sulk about how badly my race had gone. What's the point in celebrating? Our parents were delighted that Alistair was World Junior Champ; I felt like no one even wanted to talk about my race. It taught me an important lesson: we all have bad races, and you need to move on from them.

SWIM

WHY SWIM?

ALISTAIR The sensation of swimming well is unlike anything else. It feels entirely natural for you to be in the water and moving easily through it, your rhythm relaxed and consistent. You can dive in and just know from the first few strokes that, today, it will all work – your feel for the water, the way your hands and arms grip it, the way your body slides through it. Everything just feels right.

In a pool there is little to see; swimming in open water tears away the blinkers, and suddenly you have a world of visual stimulus, just as you do when out on your bike or running through the countryside. The perfect swim in Britain is in Semerwater: a warm sunny day, no wetsuit required, the water flat and still. The perfect swim anywhere you could choose would be in a tropical sea, from beach out to an island and back, looking down as you stroke to see stingrays. Swimming there, surrounded by fish, warm salt water keeping you buoyant, you are alone with your thoughts yet entirely happy with them. There is nothing to compare with that.

WHY WE SWIM AS WE DO

ALISTAIR Some Olympic athletes' training programmes are the result of hundreds of hours of lab tests, sports science degrees and computer-generated forecasts. Ours are far more prosaic: a mixture of history, environment and random experiment.

Being brought up just outside Leeds was the key factor. It was a little like accidentally winning the triathlon lottery: there was access to good swimming pools and great swimming clubs like City of Leeds and City of Bradford; there were great running routes; endless cycling routes, and a culture of both running and cycling that goes back decades and will continue for years to come.

JONNY We race mainly over the Olympic, or standard, distance: a 1,500 metre swim, 40 kilometre bike and 10 kilometre run. To cope with that, over the course of a normal training week we can swim an average of 20,000 metres, split over five different sessions. These start at seven a.m., which in many ways is an ideal time – not so early that we're a mess for the rest of the day, not so late that we can't squeeze in all the rest of our training during daylight hours.

It also means that we can swim with the main group of

triathletes based in Leeds. Much later and the pools are in use by other groups. But it would be wonderful to train with pure swimmers, simply because we could learn so much from them. We benefit from cycling with hard-core bikers and running with pure 5 kilometre and 10 kilometre lads, and the same would be true in the water. Even from training with the best swimmer in elite triathlon, our Slovakian friend Richard Varga, my stroke has improved a great deal.

Since we race in open water, you might think we train in it too. Sadly, we don't. It's not practical. As kids we went up to Ilkley in the summer and swam in the River Wharfe, and as teenagers we went to Otley Lakes. I loved it. There was a Monday night race series in the lakes where it would be so dark by the end that you'd have to stop at each buoy and peer into the distance to try to work out where you were meant to be going. You'd swim round an island, have a fight with a swan and swim back. Now that's swimming.

THE HARD YARDS

JONNY Of the three main elements to our training, swimming is the one that is toughest on the brain. With running and biking you achieve something by physically going somewhere. With swimming you don't. All you can do is stare at the tiles going past or the black line stretching out in front of you. The only sense of achievement comes from completing your set.

The hardest aspect of this toughest element is the timing of it. Swimming at seven a.m. means getting up no later than six thirty. Your bed at that hour is a delight – warm, cosy, dark. The pool is cold, wet and noisy. Even the house is cold, let alone the car, the walk from the car, then the changing rooms. You can see us all on the side of the pool as the sun comes up, doing anything but get on with it. You'll ask the coach what the warm-up is, and then two minutes later you ask him again.

ALISTAIR Getting up early is the one thing I really hate about training – you're tired, you're aching, all you can think about is sleep. But the strange thing is that all that worrying, all that fear of the cold, it all goes within ten strokes of diving in. It's forgotten. You're doing it.

The key trick for me is remembering that it's part of my routine. Getting to the swimming pool early in the morning is just what you do, and then there's someone there telling you what to do; it's a squad event, and you dive in and do it. If I missed that squad session and turned up at the pool by myself, I'd stand on the side and prevaricate: hmm, five hundred metres to do, and that's just the warm-up, then I've got three thousand metres more to do . . . I'd just about get to 2,000 metres and then I'd think: I can't be bothered with this, and get out.

I'm unbelievably motivated for almost everything, but swimming I find really hard. I've got better as I've got older. But it's so hard to do it by yourself. You can try writing the session on a piece of paper and sticking it on the poolside, but nothing works as well as having a coach there writing it on a whiteboard, telling you what to do, with the rest of your group all there with you. That way you don't make the association between where you are and what you have to do; you're just diving in, following instructions, not thinking about it.

JONNY It tells you something about the sort of mentality I have that, once I've got over the pain of getting out of bed and into the pool, I actually like that feeling of getting the early session done. It might be the session that I enjoy the least, but it's fixed: you know the location; you know how long it's going to take.

To get through it, morning after morning, you really need a good group around you. Everyone has to be into it together. And everything has to be broken into chunks and sub-sets. Even your warm-up will be broken into discrete elements – 800 metres, broken up into 200 metre front crawl, 200 metre backstroke, 200 metre drills, 200 metre kicks. You'll be standing at the end of a lane, and the coach will shout, 'Go in ten seconds!' You don't have the chance to think about it. You don't have to think ahead, you don't have to worry about the 4,000 metres to come. Dive in, do the warm-up, do the first set. It takes care of itself.

ALISTAIR When you can swim in open water it's brilliant. It's so much more interesting, so much more fun, but in the UK it does tend to be somewhat cold. I remember as a young teenager going on a training camp that took us swimming at Salford Quays. The water was nine degrees – we were so cold we couldn't take our wetsuits off afterwards. We had to stand in the showers desperately trying to warm up, and then the coach would tell us to get back in. We couldn't open our hands. It was awful.

THE SECRET OF TRIATHLON SWIMMING

JONNY You ride your bike or you run lots and you're going to get faster. Swimming isn't like that. Instead there's a trade-off between how good you are technically and how much you can do.

Swimming for triathlon is very different from swimming in a pool. You don't want the perfect stroke, because you're not swimming alone in a pristine pool lane. You're being bashed around, beaten up, thumped by waves.

ALISTAIR It's a catch-22. You need to do a lot of swimming to develop the strength to have a good stroke, so you have a long reach and a good catch. But doing too much swimming can also ruin your stroke. And there's no point in practising a perfect stroke at slow, controlled speeds because as soon as you step on the gas it will all fall apart.

In races you shouldn't be trying to go as fast as you can. That will sound strange, but it's about conserving as much energy as possible while not losing out. That's why we spend one of our main swimming sessions doing endless lots of 100 metres at 1 minute 10 seconds pace. The aim is to be able to swim at about those speeds in a race, but as easily as possible, with as little exertion as you can. And you adjust your stroke around that. You make a small tweak and then watch the clock as you swim to see what difference it makes. How easily can you swim 1,500 metres at the pace of 1 minute 10 seconds per 100 metres? That's the key question for a pro, because you'll never have to swim much faster than that in a race.

Neither Jonny nor I is a particularly powerful athlete. A lot of tri coaching tells you that the fewer strokes you take the better. Not for us. I swim best when I'm fit. It's as simple as that. I don't swim off a powerful stroke, or a long stroke, but on arm turnover – the number of strokes I can take per minute. It's the same on the bike. I don't have enormous power, but I can create a very fast cadence on the pedals. The fitter I am, the easier that is.

It does help that we've been swimming since the age of four. Our techniques really shouldn't require too much work. But I also think that swimming properly for triathlon is something that not many people in the world genuinely understand, if that.

The secret is all about the efficiency, whether you're a pro, beginner or improver. That's the big difference in a race between the swim and the run. The first you're just trying to get through as easily as possible; the last you're trying to do as fast as you can. So few people understand that.

I'll make this complicated for a moment. The most important technical thing about triathlon swimming is the ratio between your threshold speed and your maximum speed. If your maximum speed is really fast and your threshold speed – roughly speaking, the point where your muscles start producing more lactic acid than they can get rid of, and so causing horrible pain and an unarguable slowing – is not close to it you're in huge trouble. Because it means that, while you can go out really hard over the first 300 metres, you can't maintain it. You'll blow up. You're so far in the red that you have to drop your pace to a very low level to be able to recover.

There are three types of swimmer in triathlon: those that have a relatively high maximum speed to a lower threshold speed; those with a relatively low max speed to a higher threshold; those that have a low maximum and a low threshold speed. Triathletes from the first and last groups often perform remarkably similarly in races, even though on paper those from the first are much better swimmers.

You'll see some swimmers who are very fast in a pool but haven't developed the ability to swim efficiently at pace over long distances. They've trained at a really high pace all the time. They'll go out hard and use up all their strength too fast, which is why there is generally a dead spot in tri races at about 300 metres or 400 metres. That's where the initial madness slows down and sorts itself out. Before then you'll have people you've overtaken coming back past you for a brief moment of glory before it settles down.

Because Jonny and I don't have loads of power, we can't go really fast and so we can't go into the red. And as it turns out – completely by fluke – that makes us ideal for triathlon swimming. I'm not sure we could get much faster even if we swam to the exclusion of everything else. We don't have big enough shoulders, and we're not six foot five. There's a biological cap on it.

Someone could come along who could swim a minute faster than us and bike well too. But they may not be able to run at the end of it all. And if you are a faster swimmer – like

Javier Gomez is – it can actually work against you, because your rivals can settle in behind your feet and get a lovely tow off you. It might change our tactics a little if there were two or three who could do it, who could maybe get away and so force us to swim harder. And if three or four could swim and bike very fast we could be in trouble. But I hope we wouldn't be far enough off the front for it to truly cost us overall.

HOW TO IMPROVE YOUR SWIMMING

ALISTAIR First things first. We swim in pools of all lengths. Swim where you can, when you can. Make your swimming part of your routine, by going before work, or at lunchtime, so it isn't hanging over you all day. Swim with friends when it's possible – it's more fun, and you won't notice the effort; or train with a triathlon or swim club. Swim the majority of your session front crawl – you can certainly complete your first tri doing breaststroke, but crawl is far more efficient. Mix up the strokes in your warm-up and cool-down. And if you're really struggling for motivation, remind yourself why you're doing it. Each session counts. Break the session into manageable chunks; put a bottle of water pool-side; use the time to focus on your technique; enjoy the sensation of swimming well, rather than being stuck at work or behind a desk.

There should be three key paces that you aim to cover in your tri-swim training plan.

- **Speed swimming.** For most good amateur triathletes, your top speed isn't actually a big factor in races. Think of it as the pace you would want to swim the first 100/200 metres of a 1,500 metre swim to get out from the pack fast.
- **Threshold swimming.** Your perfect race pace once you have settled into a rhythm.
- **Aerobic endurance swimming.** A steady pace usually around 10–20 seconds per 100 metres slower than your threshold.

If you're swimming three times a week, do at least one threshold and one aerobic endurance session every week, and a speed session every two weeks. Throw in some technique drills in your warm-up, and be sensible with your time and energy: three 45-minute sessions are better than two one-hour ones.

Coaches' Corner

Here's an example of a great swim session. Each swimmer has their own strengths and weaknesses, so your own training programme should reflect your unique level, but you can use this as a guide. We'll work on the basis that a 1,500 metre swim takes you 25 minutes, but you can tweak both the speed and distance according to your own abilities.

1. 500 metres warm-up. Keep it slow, mix up your strokes, concentrate on technique.
2. 8 x 50 metres drills. Select drills specific to your weaknesses.
3. 4 x 50 metres build – increase the pace gradually over those 50 metres.
4. 5 x 100 metres swim – the first 100 metres steady, the second a little harder, the third harder still, the fourth at your racing pace and the fifth slightly faster.
5. Repeat that last block twice more, so you have swum 1,500 metres.
6. 200 metres cool-down.

The Big Time

ALISTAIR

A month after the World Juniors, I went off for my first term at Cambridge. It felt wrong from the moment I arrived.

I'd had a chat with my mum and dad before I went. The thinking was: at least go and try it – you might be able to do both; that might be your cup of tea. Perhaps you could do your pre-clinical, take time out to try for the 2012 Olympics and then go back for your clinical. You might even like the academic side of things more than sport. I really enjoyed studying at school. But I also think my parents believed that if they could get me there I might stay.

I'd always associated success in sport with working really hard. I'd won the English Schools because I trained really hard for it, and I won the World Junior Championships because I trained really hard for it. But I'd never felt the same way about academic stuff. I'd never felt like it was a goal, and I'd never had to work that hard at it. I'd just fallen into it – I did well at my A-Levels without too much work because I went to a good school and they taught me how to do it. I'd never do any work at home, because I had a bag that was so small you could cycle with it, but you couldn't fit a book in it. What do you do if you're clever at school? Medicine. My teacher told me I should apply, so I did; but I never did any extra practice and I just rocked up to the interview. So Cambridge couldn't feel like a big deal for me, because I hadn't focused on it or worked hard for it.

I made a conscious effort to enjoy myself, because I knew it was a unique experience, but the life of an international triathlete soon rubbed up against that of an undergraduate. I wanted to keep my bike in my room, because it was worth £2,000, but that broke the protocol and they told me off – they wanted me to keep it in the sheds. I had nowhere to park my car; I was going swimming at five a.m. down at Parker's Piece but at first I wasn't allowed a car to get there. My supervision – what they call a tutorial at Cambridge – might suddenly be changed from mid-afternoon to the evening, when I was supposed to be at swim training, and there was never much of a question in my mind as to which would get the chop.

Something had to change, and it was Cambridge. Initially I thought about deferring my place until I'd seen how the sport went, and Girton College was good about that.

I spoke to my parents during those Christmas holidays. They were definitely disappointed, Mum a lot more so than Dad. It was almost impossible for Mum to understand my logic: she's a conventional person, and she would have given anything to be able to go to Cambridge to study medicine. But both she and Dad knew I wasn't very happy.

Dad sat me down and asked me what I was going to do. I told him that I didn't know, but I did know that I wasn't happy at that moment. And he said, in not so many words, that I had to follow my dreams, that I had to follow a path I would enjoy. His attitude was that, whatever you do, you must make sure you commit to it. And if you commit to what you're doing and do it to the best of your ability, that's all you can ask for.

It can't have been an easy thing for him to say. Dad didn't understand triathlon too well; he'd always been involved in medicine. It also meant that I would be going back to living at Mum and Dad's, and that I might be there for a long time.

I know from what Jonny said that they were both very stressed around that time. Jonny and Ed would look at each other as the discussion built around the kitchen table and think: right, maybe we should go to our rooms . . .

For me it was one of the pivotal points of my life. Being at Cambridge helped me realize that sport was what I wanted to do; leaving Cambridge was really committing myself to it. It was symbolic: as one future closed off, so another opened. From now on, there could be no more doubt about it. I wanted to try to be as good as I could.

Back in my home city other changes were happening behind the scenes that would help me on my new path. The British Triathlon Federation had nominated Leeds as one of its dedicated performance centres, which meant that as soon as I returned from Cambridge there was a swim squad I could train with, and when the central funding was cut back, Leeds Met University decided to step in and make up the shortfall, with my coach Malcolm at the helm.

British Triathlon could have messed things up at that point. All the pressure from them was to get me to move to their main performance centre in Loughborough, but I fought it tooth and nail because I knew what a massive mistake that would be. Leeds is where I train best. I might have been okay with swimming squads elsewhere, but not with the biking and running squads. I knew training partners, I knew training routes, and I knew it worked.

Coaches were ringing up from universities in Bath and Swansea, offering me places that I did consider, but it had to be Leeds. The BTF kept at it, too – at one point they wanted me to go down to Loughborough every two weeks, because they wanted to keep an eye on me. But that idea lasted only a month or so, because I just wouldn't answer their phone calls.

The BTF, partly influenced by the success British Cycling has had since it established the National Cycling Centre, had decided to centralize its performance and funding, focusing its resources in Loughborough. This has meant dismantling the regional camp system that Jonny and I benefited from so much. I'm far from convinced that centralization works for triathlon. As with other sports, the real test is whether there are any real podium-level athletes in these national training centres. Cycling is the case where it worked, but that doesn't mean the model should be applied to all sports. My argument has always been, why change something if it's working for you?

I believe that the characters who are strong enough to succeed outside the system will be good enough to make it. The basis for a lot of success is that you take ownership of what you do. You choose the elements that you want around you; you build the community and support system that you want. If you can make those decisions yourself it makes you stronger. And that helps you race well. You stand on the start line and think: I'm one hundred per cent responsible for what I do here.

But the minute you take those decisions away from athletes it's really dangerous. When they don't do well they begin to think their coach is partly responsible, and then already they are making an excuse for failure. But the buck should always stop with you.

The common theme with a lot of successful athletes is that they have made their own decisions and picked their own coaches. Look at double Olympic Champion Mo Farah and 400 metre hurdles World Champion Dai Greene. Both have found their greatest success by operating independently of UK Athletics' two main training centres, using their own coaches and making their own decisions.

I think a lot of people at the BTF have realized that successful performance isn't about forcing things on athletes; it's about removing restrictions. I'm sure those in charge back then thought a move to a centre like Loughborough was in my best interests, even when it wasn't.

Triathlon requires a lot of training, 70 per cent of which is outdoors. Therefore your physical environment becomes the key factor. The other stuff – access to sports medicine, strength and conditioning, nutrition and, worst of all, sports psychology – accounts for less than 5 per cent of your performance.

A governing body's elite performance plan should be about providing a safety net while removing barriers to success, rather than putting obstacles in the way. Fortunately, for the last two years, that's how it has been for us. We are in charge of what we do; we take responsibility for our training and its end performance.

So, as my own boss, fully aware what I would have to do, I began to work on making the move from successful junior to competitive senior. I won the 2007 European Juniors comfortably and was taking aim at the Worlds when, cycling out in the Pyrenees a couple of weeks before the competition, I was hit by a motorbike, head on, as I came round a mountain bend. Bang. I was knocked unconscious, woke up flat on the ground and then jumped up thinking I was okay, only to realize I couldn't move my arms. It was the strangest feeling: had that really just happened? When would movement return?

Typically, though, I tried swimming in the lake that afternoon, just using one arm and my legs, and over the next few days I gradually began to recover. My shoulders were still sore, but when I managed to raise my arms above my head I knew I could compete at the Worlds. I didn't win it – Aurélien Raphaël did, after I missed a breakaway of five athletes on the bike. There was, inevitably, disappointment that I hadn't won it. But, equally, I'd done well from an unpromising position, coming through fast on the run, and Aurélien was a great triathlete.

It might seem strange that many promising juniors have not gone on to have the same success as seniors. If they could beat me then, why couldn't they beat me now? Well, a lot of those good juniors were big, strong, powerful teenagers, but at junior level you're racing for an hour in total – and the run is only 5 kilometres. At elite level you need to be a pure endurance athlete, which is a big jump to make. You have to get through an hour and twenty minutes of racing before you even run, and that's where their struggles begin.

I looked for my next target. At the end of the 2007 season I got the chance to race in an ITU World Cup event in Rhodes. It was late in the year and so the quality of the field wasn't as good as it could have been, but it was still a first chance to test myself against the big boys of global triathlon, and I was massively excited about it.

It was still only my fourth Olympic-distance race (1,500 metres swim, 40 kilometre bike, 10 kilometre run), but I took a gamble on the bike and decided to break away. There were two guys away up the road already, so a racer called Sven Riederer, bronze medallist in Athens, and I gave chase. Even to be working with Sven felt amazing. He was a big fast fish, one of the big names on the scene, one of those I had watched from afar on television.

We came off the bike and into the run and very quickly we hauled in Kris Gemmell, who had the lead. It wasn't to be a fairy-tale debut – Kris out-sprinted me on the line to snatch the win – but to come second in a World Cup race was a huge thing for me at that point. The big British names were there: Will Clarke was racing, Stuart Hayes was racing. Beating those established names felt good. But at that stage it wasn't everything, and even then, having raced myself into the ground for an hour and forty-five minutes, I was nagged by the thought that maybe I'd given up at the end. Maybe I should have pushed harder.

The last minute haunted me. But that performance turned out to be hugely significant, because it meant that although I began 2008 with some poor races, I was still eligible for the qualifying race for the Olympics. And that was the start of a whole new level.

There were other signs that my form was coming good. Two weeks before Rhodes I raced in the final French Grand Prix race of the summer.

I came off the bike and ran really hard for the first 2.5 kilometres. There were just four of us – reigning World Champion Javier Gómez, Will Clarke, Stuart Hayes and me. I thought: wow! I'm running with Gomez!

At 3 kilometres he suddenly put in a massive surge, and I went after him. It felt as if I was sprinting flat out just to stay with him. One thought kept hammering round my brain: go for it, go for it, go for it.

Will and Stu were dropped. But it couldn't last – I went flat out for 3 kilometres, following Gomez stride for stride, and then went backwards. Will and Stu came through to beat me in a sprint finish on the line. But to me that wasn't the point. I tried to go with the best runner in the world, at a time when he was dominating everything, at a time when no one else would have even considered it.

That winter should have been great, but instead it was miserable. Everything that could go wrong did. I picked up a hip injury, crashed my bike, got a chain ring stuck in my calf and went down to Australasia where I raced with utterly limited success. But there was a prize on the horizon. When I came home at the start of 2008 I knew I had six weeks until Madrid, the final qualifying race for the British team at the Beijing

Olympics. I shouldn't have felt confident. I had only just managed to scrape into the field for the race because of my performance in Rhodes at the end of the previous season; I'd come in twelfth at the European Championships the previous month and fifth in the Grand Prix at Dunkirk the week before.

Those results suggested I wasn't in any great form, certainly not in the sort of shape required. I needed to finish in the top eight overall to have any chance of qualifying, and then be one of the first three Britons home. But I sensed that everyone there was very stressed about it, because no one had pre-qualified; rather pleasantly, that meant I didn't feel the same pressure. Tim Don and Will Clarke were the main men at the time. I was just there to race. No one expected anything of me, and there was nothing there to intimidate me.

Coming out of the swim I was in good shape and a good place. Then, from nowhere, there was the most torrential rain storm Madrid had ever seen. The whole of transition was under water. The blue carpet was floating away. They were within a few droplets of calling the whole thing off.

I looked around, and the possibilities were suddenly clear. Olly Freeman, another of the young Brits, was nowhere – the occasion had got to him. Andrew Johns was gone too – too cold, out of the race. That left four of us: Tim, Will, Stuart Hayes and me. Stu then got a double puncture. Three of us, and now a top-eight finish gets me to the Olympics. I've almost qualified by default . . . Oh shit.

You'd think that the national coaches would maintain their neutrality when it came to qualification, but I'm not certain that happened. I could hear Tim's coach shouting, 'Alistair's only five seconds ahead of you – you have to catch him!' And I could hear Will's coach – the national men's coach – shouting, 'Alistair's only twenty seconds ahead – you've got to catch him!' I thought:

that's not very fair. And then a moment later: there's no chance you're catching me! It was a wonderful motivator.

Jumping off the bike I felt great. I ran with Gomez for the first 2 kilometres again, let him go, and then stayed as close as I could. Tim was chasing me down, and I hung in and hung in . . . and hung on to third.

I was going to my first Olympics at the age of twenty. I'd come third in a World Cup race, I'd beaten the best two Brits, I'd kept it together when lots of others had lost it.

JONNY

When Alistair moved out of my age group, it created space that allowed me to come through.

I went to the World Juniors on the Gold Coast in 2009 with real expectation that I could win. I was nineteen now, the peak age for it, and the previous year in Vancouver I'd come third with the two guys ahead of me both older and so out of the reckoning the following year. I'd had some success in the few senior races I'd tried that year too – coming second in one of the French Grand Prix, which was considered quite favourably – and I was coming off the back of a comfy win at the European Championships.

We were sent to a holding-camp in Sailfish Cove. It was one of the first times I had stayed in a different apartment to Alistair, and I had to cook for myself. Since I had no idea how, this was perhaps not a great shout. Over the next two weeks I lost quite a bit of weight, which may well have had a bearing on what happened next.

The race was at Surfer's Paradise. My swim was good, the bike felt awful but had me in contention and I managed to build a small lead into the run. That's where it all began to go wrong. Mario Mola of Spain, always a good runner, came past me with a kilometre to go, and suddenly I began to feel terrible. In the course of a couple of minutes I went from winning the thing into survival mode. I managed to hang on to second. Only just.

Did I celebrate? Not in the usual manner. I'd felt progressively worse over that final kilometre of the run, and as I stood on the podium waiting to collect my medal I was aware that the entire world had started tilting sideways.

All I could think was, let this presentation end now, I'm about to collapse. Instead I was asked to do a television interview. I just about managed to get the words out to tell them I couldn't, only to be told I had no choice. So as the first question came ('How did you find the race?'), I went sideways and blacked out.

I came back to consciousness lying on a stretcher with wires sticking out of me. That was the good news. The bad was that my heart was behaving strangely, and the doctors told me that I might never be able to do sport again.

It was the most awful thing I've experienced. My dad, as a doctor, was also fearing the worst. I was sent for ultrasound on my heart, an ECG, and then an MRI, all of which were terrifying. A big part of me wanted to ignore the whole thing, and just carry on regardless as if nothing had ever happened. Dad insisted I had the scans done, only to suddenly change his mind when he arrived to take me to the hospital.

'Are you sure you want to do this? If you hear there's something wrong, will you carry on doing sport anyway?'

I told him I would. He looked at me, shook his head and said, 'So what's the point?'

I lay in the dreadful MRI machine, that awful tunnel, for what seemed like an age. It works off your heart rate. Typically the sort of people who go through there are old, often women, with resting heartbeat of 80 beats per minute. Mine's 38. I was in there for four hours.

You get some great doctors who really understand our sport, and they understand how your brain works as an athlete. Then you have others who have no idea at all how important it all is to you. It was the latter. As I came out of the scan I asked one doctor when we'd get the results. 'Oh, two weeks or so.' All I could think was, two weeks without training?

I still trained hard during that fortnight. My predominant thought was this: if I did have a potentially fatal heart defect, would I actually want to know? The answer was simple. I would want to train hard regardless. If I die doing sport, then so be it.

When the results came through, I was in the clear. My heart was big, and healthy, and back to where it should be. Relief? Alistair was very sympathetic. 'I'm not running with you,' he told me, 'in case you drop dead halfway round.'

The mental pain of not winning that race stuck around. You have limited chances to win a World Junior title. Once that twentieth birthday ticks round, it's gone. So 2009 was supposed to be my big year. Alistair had been champion; I thought I had to be. To make it worse, Alistair won the senior World Championship that weekend. Again I felt completely overshadowed. I felt like a failure. 'You're not that good, because you're not World Junior Champion.'

Because Alistair's victories were there for all to see, it was hard for me to think of them as anything but inevitable. There could be no 'Well, it only happened because someone else had a bad bike, or was injured.' They were historical fact. What it meant was that I worked even harder to match him. All I could see was unbroken success for him, and me falling just short. There was only one way to deal with that: work harder.

From that point on the Gold Coast I knew I had at least

something. I didn't quite know if it would ever translate into anything at senior level, but with each good result came a growing sense of confidence.

The big breakthrough for me at the top level came in the Hyde Park race of 2010. People remember it for Alistair collapsing across the line rather than for my senior debut, but it was the start of the final assault on the summit for me. I genuinely feared I would never be able to make the step up into the seniors; I'd had a shocking race at the European Championships earlier that summer, so being able to race hard in London and come second made me start to believe that I actually had what it took.

For once I had out-performed Alistair. At the age I was coming second in London, he had qualified for the Olympics in Beijing, but he had never got close to such a good result in a World Series event.

Yet his collapse meant, once again, that he was the big story rather than me. The media were interested only in him, while our parents were obviously upset about the state he was in. Their primary focus after the race was making sure he was okay rather than celebrating with me. If it was something I was having to get used to, it didn't make it any easier. But, once again, it spurred me on.

Had everyone been telling me I was the business, I may have sat back, even if just a little. That I was ignored made me want to prove everyone wrong, and gave me an even higher target to strive for.

Once I reached that top level, it all happened rather quickly. I had been a junior in 2009, but after London I was able to establish myself as a senior much more quickly than I had thought possible.

Part of the battle was mental. I found that the easiest way of coping with the concern about whether I was good enough was simply not to think about it – to push it to the back of my mind, and let my physical abilities take me where they would.

It might sound like I resented my brother. I didn't, and I don't. Having Alistair around me made that transition up to the top level so much easier.

You always imagine that the world champion must do incredible things. You think that his training must be at an entirely different level to yours, that he must be doing superhuman splits in the pool or on the track. To be able to train with that world champion is one huge advantage; he tows you round to faster times and better performances.

To live with him takes it to a new level. You realize that, if the world champion is eating ordinary food, then so can you. If the world champion eats fish and chips for tea, you can too. If the world champion comes from a little town just outside Leeds, then you can be that world champion too. For someone as intense as me, these were invaluable lessons.

On Top of the World

ALISTAIR

I was genuinely surprised I qualified for the 2008 Olympics. I was such an outsider. But I was coming into some wonderful form.

In Vancouver a few weeks later I won the World Under-23 Championships, and then I went straight away on British Triathlon camps, first to Austin in Texas to get used to the heat they expected us to face in Beijing. Strange things happened there. We were given microscopic thermometers in pill form and told to swallow them so they could monitor our core temperature. There was a rumour that we would have to re-use them for budget reasons, but I'm glad to say it turned out to be exactly that – a rumour. I was in the prep camp in Korea almost before I'd had time to think about it.

Somewhere along the way my expectation changed from just wanting to qualify to thinking: I could be top thirty in the world . . . or top twenty . . . or top ten . . . maybe I could win. I'm not sure I was thinking that clearly, but there was a belief I could do really well. Which was daft; I shouldn't have had a chance in hell.

The Olympics were utterly different to anything I'd ever experienced before. I'd never done a press conference. I'd never been to Beijing, when all my rivals had been there and raced on that course. I know how some athletes find themselves overwhelmed by it all at their first Games. Going to the village and seeing all these big stars! I was blown away.

But I knew I could keep that sense of being there to race. When I had raced so dreadfully at those first World Juniors Malcolm and I had vowed that I would never again go away and race that badly. From then on I always had in my mind that it could never be just about being there. You were there to perform.

If anything I found it all felt strangely familiar. It was an Olympic triathlon, but it was still a triathlon. The same guy was there introducing us to the crowd. The race briefing was the same. The course was a standard, unexciting course. We were so far out of Beijing that little of the Olympic glamour made it out there.

I had absolutely no strategy in my brain when I stood there on the pontoon before the hooter. The closest I had to that was a simple, 'Go for it.' I was prepared to be brave and risk everything to do well, because I was fairly confident I couldn't win by simply out-running people or waiting for others to fail. My dad kept saying to me, 'Fortune favours the brave, Alistair!', and I knew that to do really well I had to put myself in a good position. And that's what I tried to do.

The swim was fine. On the bike I decided to try to get away, but not much happened – until I hit the run, when suddenly I felt absolutely amazing.

It was ridiculous! I've never again felt so good. All I could think was, I'm having the best day of my entire life, and it's the Olympics. It felt as if I was jogging. That's how easy it was.

There were four laps. We went through the finish area the first time, past the big grandstands, and the hairs were standing up on my arms because it felt so spookily easy. I felt super-aware of everything around me, and that's always a good sign for me because it shows that I'm not trying that hard.

At the end of the second three of us broke away from the

rest. I was just starting to hurt a little. Coming into the third lap I missed getting my water bottle from the feed station because the New Zealander Bevan Docherty ran straight up my inside on purpose to stop me getting it.

I found out afterwards that Jonny, watching on from the stands, felt rather differently about it: 'I hope Alistair doesn't win, because he will be so boring about it. Olympic champions are supposed to be the best! They're not my brother.' If that seems uncharitable, it was also illogical. If I won, I would be showing that someone from his exact background, with precisely his training, could be the best in the world.

Coming back up the hill on lap three it all suddenly became immaterial. My legs went, and they went very quickly. After that it almost immediately became a survival mission. I went from racing mode to just trying to finish. I've never before or since gone from feeling so good to so bad so quickly.

What happened? I'm not sure I knew how fast I was going early on. I wasn't aware how much it was taking out of me. The heat too played a role. Had I been a little more conservative all the way through I'm sure I could have held on a lot longer. But once you overheat you overheat. I sat in the athletes' area afterwards and felt so hot that I had to climb into one of the big tubs of cold water and ice that hold the Coca-Cola. I stuck my head in it and the rest of me just followed in.

JONNY

Just as Alistair was having his own Olympic debut in Beijing, so I was getting my first taste of what might come in London.

With a few other lucky teenagers, I had been flown out to watch those 2008 Games as part of 2012 Olympic Ambition, a programme for promising young British athletes. We were taken to the official Team GB holding-camp in Macau, where my overriding memory is of being allowed to order drinks in the hotel whenever we wanted them. I was quite amazed.

The young boxers on the trip did nothing but cause trouble. Visits to unusual massage places. A lot went on. They seemed to go around punching walls. I'm not sure whether it was training, instinct or a sense of competition, but there would be fist-shaped holes in the walls wherever we went. Complaints would come in from officials, who just couldn't understand it. Neither did their coaches. That was my first Olympics lesson: never rent out a house to a boxer.

We arrived in Beijing only a day before the triathlon. We were given a museum-style tour of the athletes' village – 'This is where they eat; this is where they swim' – and even there we were innocents abroad. There were issues getting to the race, which was miles out of town. The taxi drivers had no idea where it was; we had the address written down in Cantonese, but it made no difference. The taxi out there cost £2; the one to come back cost £50.

I had several shocks as the race began. There were people trying to buy tickets to watch triathlon, which came as a surprise. When I tried to sit with our coaches, Malcolm Brown was pacing up and down, nervous as anything, unable to speak to me, and Jack Maitland spent most of it chatting up a girl. Then, to my disbelief, my brother not only took the lead but appeared until quite late in the run to be about to win the thing. I was disgusted. 'This is the Olympics. It's special. You can't have my brother winning it!'

ALISTAIR

I never made the mental leap ahead to what that lead might mean. I never let myself think that I might actually steal it. And at the finish line all I could think was: what the hell did I just do? What an absolute idiot! You were winning the Olympics with 7 kilometres of a 10 kilometre run done, nine-tenths of the way through the entire race, and you've gone from there to twelfth?

I came round pretty quickly. Earlier in the year I'd come twelfth in the European Championships, and here I was coming twelfth at the Olympics. I didn't spend too much time worrying about what might have happened had I raced it differently. You have to go out there to try to win a medal, and that's what I did. Had I raced differently I might have come fourth or fifth, but I don't see that as anything better. I raced with the best in the world until 7 kilometres on the run, and that gave me a lot of confidence for the season ahead.

From small moments come great things. If I hadn't held on in Madrid I wouldn't have gone to the Olympics. If I hadn't led in Beijing I wouldn't have had the confidence to go out and achieve what I did in 2009. I'm sure I would have been the same athlete physically. But mentally I wouldn't have had the self-belief to race in the same way. And I'm not sure I would have had the motivation. Beijing gave me a huge kick because I realized how close I was to the top. I was already 95 per cent of the way there.

I've always thought that your mental ability is a secondary skill. If you're fit enough, nothing else matters. When I won the first World Series race of 2009 I thought my mental state was irrelevant. But who knows? Beijing transformed me from someone who thought it was great to be among the ten best seniors to someone who realized they could be the best.

It all happened so quickly. Bang – qualifying for the Europeans. Bang – qualifying for the Olympics. Bang – leading in Beijing for so long, and then opening out the next season as the best triathlete, at that moment, in the world.

That first race of 2009 was a massive shock: suddenly I'm beating everyone. I'd spent that winter absolutely working my backside off. I was at home, training consistently, even if the training that I had done before the Olympics dwarfed it in terms of volume and quality. But this was the big jump for me.

I went from barely expecting to race, to getting a place in the big fields, to probably winning them, to everyone expecting me to. You have to deal with the fact that everyone is now watching you. You have to adjust your tactics in the race. I'm not sure I enjoyed it at first.

I won the World Series events in Madrid, Washington and Kitzbühel, and the fourth was London. It was the first time we had raced on what would be the Olympic course in Hyde Park. I was a twenty-one-year-old with three consecutive big race wins behind me, and the change was impossible to miss. I became aware, for the first time, that my name was being linked to an Olympic gold medal in London three years further on.

The pressure was suddenly crushing me. I looked around and thought: wow – not only does everyone expect me to win, but they think winning is an inevitable outcome. They think I just turn up and win, rather than appreciating just what a fine line there is.

I'd been the underdog. I was a great underdog. I would make those crazy moves to win races and inevitably fail, albeit in a glorious, devil-may-care fashion. When the wins first came there were always reasons why this skinny underdog had somehow pulled it off – in Madrid I got in the key bike breakaway, and it was a hilly course – 'Ah, that suits him,' they'd say. I won in Washington by being in a breakaway of five. I flogged myself into the dirt to keep us away, the hardest thing I'd ever done, and I stayed away on the run. The whispers were the same: 'Ah, you only won because you made the breakaway.' Hang on, I thought – I've battered myself with a 40 kilometre time trial, that's how I've done it. But people tell themselves what they want to hear. I was winning in ways that no one expected.

Gomez beat me at the European Championships. A week later, in Kitzbühel, we went head to head and I beat him again. Now people started changing their tune. They could no longer pretend that this was some sort of fluke.

Four races in, we headed to the Gold Coast with a simple sum ahead of me: finish fifth or higher, and you become world champion.

Simple sum it might have been, but it began to mess with me. On one level I couldn't stop thinking how amazing it all was. Then the doubts began to creep in – what if I crash? What if I puncture? What if I can't get my shoe on properly? All these stupid little things that I hadn't given a second's thought to before.

On the start line, clarity returned. Alistair, what are you doing thinking about finishing fifth? You cannot race with the intention of coming fifth. You just have to go out there and race as hard as you can. But I had walked on to the pontoon thinking of the world title as being mine to lose. I had to push that to one side and think instead of that sporting cliché that contains so much truth: control the controllables. Don't obsess over a possible puncture. If it happens there is nothing you can do about it. Make it simple. Go out there and try to win.

I won.

I remain intensely proud of my performance. I had to give everything I had, empty everything out, to win that race. It was so close on the run – Gomez would attack me mercilessly, time and time again, and I would force myself to fight back past him, just to show him I could. I'd never before been in a battle that was so psychological.

He threw in one final immense attack on the hill on the third lap. I went past him at the top, glanced at his face and knew in that instant that I'd won. Before then I'd thought those moments never happen. I thought people always raced all the way to the line, that it wasn't about the head but about how fast you are. But in that momentary glance, it was there for me to see: he has lost the race, right here. We ran together for the rest of the lap. But it was over.

I wound it up from 1,500 metres out, pushed on, and came round the final corner, 400 metres from the finish, thinking that if he came round my shoulder then I would have no more to give. But he was gone, and I was home.

The aftermath was strange. The Gold Coast is a hotbed of triathlon. There were hundreds of people there to watch, hundreds of people who knew who you were and what you'd done. And I was so glad to get home to Leeds, where no one so much as glanced at me.

Even as world champion, I found the bumps in the road kept coming. In that winter of 2009–10 I developed another stress fracture, this time in my hip. It was a nightmare to get over, not least because it was misdiagnosed for a long time. The muscles in my hip had got so tight that they pulled the femur apart, just split it.

The injury and its repercussions were tough for me to deal with. I was finally exactly where I wanted to be, on top of the world, yet I was injured.

There was this sense that, having worked so hard to get there, I had to be racing from the very start or it might all slip away from me as quickly as it had arrived. Injuries have a curious effect on your focus. You imagine yourself riding on this serendipitous wave, and that as soon as your training or racing start to drop off, you'll be dumped off the wave and be left flailing in the foam.

Can't miss a day, can't miss a session, can't miss a minute. It becomes an obsessive mantra. When you're injured it all comes crashing down. 'Alistair, you need to have five weeks off.' Wallop. Now what?

I couldn't even swim. I couldn't drive. I had to be chauffeured around by my mate Alec. We embarked on a grand tour of Yorkshire's best cafés. It was awful.

I thought I should go on holiday. It wasn't just that I had nothing to do; it was the nagging feeling that it was all disappearing from me. The fragility of success.

It was probably a great lesson for me. For one thing, I'm not sure I could have coped with the Achilles injury that hit me before the 2012 Olympics if I hadn't gone through that period in 2010. Also, at the end of 2009, I had so many people blowing smoke up my backside, telling me I was indestructible – it seemed they were almost in awe of those results – that it was probably too much.

I've always been more scared of a psychological malaise than a physical one. Break your femur, and you know that in five or six weeks it'll be better. It might be hell along the way, but you know it will mend. But a mental problem is intangible. When will you ever feel right again? When will the form return?

That period was horrendous. I'd moved into my own house for the first time, away from my parents, yet at the same time my independence was taken away from me. It was supposed to be a good time, a time for celebration. Instead I cut myself off. I just wanted to run; I just wanted to cycle. Jonny and the rest of the gang were going off, and I was left alone in this silent house.

Sport is so ingrained in me that I can lose perspective on the rest of life. When you suddenly stop exercising, you don't eat very well, you don't sleep very well. Even your toilet routine changes. When you run, it kicks your digestive system into life. When you suddenly stop, so do the pipes.

Without all that exercise I wasn't tired. So I started drinking – nothing too unhinged, just four or five pints a night on the sofa to make myself sleepy, and then that felt empty and boring too.

The sole positive about a stress fracture is that, when it's healed, you know it should stay healed. You can crack on with training. It's like when a cut on your finger heals: it's gone, I can go again. My return to training felt easy and instantaneous. And it was great – I knew I was massively unfit, but the converse of that was that every day I was feeling better and every day I was losing weight. Mind you, I expected that; with the drinking, and the inactivity, I had put on seven kilogrammes.

I'd go out for a bike ride, come back and feel fitter. As an athlete you don't feel that very often. Every improvement is so incremental that usually it's impossible to notice.

After the lows of the winter, racing in Madrid in the summer of 2010 was almost an afterthought: I've trained for a while, I've seen the same pool and roads for a while, why not? The advice was to leave it. I'd had only six weeks of running, and the start of that had been one minute of walking alternated with one minute of running. I turned up at the race under the assumption that I was underprepared. That I then won it shocked me as much as it shocked everyone else.

I managed to get into a little break on the bike about a lap and a half before the end. Somehow the gap between us and the chasing pack jumped up to two minutes, because the guys behind sat up and cruised, reasoning – with some logic – that I wasn't in any sort of shape to be a danger.

It left just two of us – me and an Australian called Courtney Atkinson – out front on the run. Everyone told me he had a sprint finish, so I decided to nail it from a minute out to see if he had anything left. He didn't. Thankfully he didn't even try to come after me.

That win felt brilliant. I had been through so much, and the memory of being stuck at home, knocking about in my new and empty house, was still so fresh. And the confidence it gives you! Standing on the pontoon before your first race back you're thinking: oh hell, I'm not fit, I can't do this. But if you can win big races off the back of so little training, what is there you can't do?

Post-Madrid it all came together in an almost dreamlike way. I had some great weeks of training, felt on top of the world and went to the European Championships to win by a mile, feeling delightfully easy.

Three weeks later, it all came crashing down again, this time literally. At the big World Series event in Hyde Park in London I collapsed in the final few metres of the run.

I still have no idea why it happened – it's still the fittest I've ever been, and I'd been flying in training. The Europeans had felt like a canter. It was hot and humid, but it's been hot and humid before; I had a dodgy stomach, but that's happened before too. Maybe it was a combination – afterwards I was puking and puking, loads of yellow gunk coming out, and that indicates I wasn't absorbing anything, including liquid.

Almost the worst thing about the collapse, apart from the fact I did it with all my family and friends watching, on live television, was the state I found myself in afterwards. I woke up in a strange tent with no memory of how I got there, and a thermometer sticking out of my arse. It was a little disconcerting.

I didn't worry about it at the time, but I should have done. A few months later I went to see a doctor who specializes in heat illnesses. Not only did he say it had been serious, but he also told me it was still serious. 'You shouldn't be racing.' My body temperature had got as high as 42 degrees, and at that point you begin to damage your cell walls. You lose proteins into your blood. We did some tests, and even then, in October, he could tell I still wasn't where I should be.

Maybe it was a good thing I didn't know. After London I could barely sleep for a week. I tried to train the day after the race, ran slowly and sideways for about ten minutes and then listened to Jonny's advice to stop. I went to Kitzbühel two weeks after London and I was appalling. That led to a holiday with Mum and Dad to France, and I thought I was gradually getting back to where I should be. But as soon as I tried to bring in some speed, or train hard enough to get really warm, my body would give up on me. I'd try harder and harder and get slower and slower.

By the time of the race in Budapest I decided my only option was to run within myself. If I red-lined at all I knew I would blow up. Coach Malcolm was on the phone, asking me if I was sure I should race. The team physio was telling me I probably shouldn't. My attitude was that, having travelled all that way, I might as well.

It was the strangest way to race. Every time I wanted to push it I had to hold back. Wherever I would usually try to break away I had to fight the urge.

Despite that, halfway through the run I looked around and it was just me and Spain's Javier Gomez left. What could I do? Usually I would wait until a kilometre to go and then kick hard,

BIKE

WHY BIKE?

JONNY Cycling is more than just pedalling for me. It's exploration. It's a day with mates. It's a rich and rewarding culture.

It began when I was a kid – pulling an Ordnance Survey map from my dad's cupboard and trying to find a destination that I could ride to, memorizing a route that I had heard was good for riding, or scribbling place names on a piece of paper and stuffing it in my back pocket. I loved the idea of cycling from busy, urban Leeds into the quiet, empty Yorkshire Dales, of covering great distances using only my own energy.

It was a social date then, and it's a social date now. When else as a triathlete can you hang out with friends and talk other than when you're out riding? When else can you spend a relaxed half-hour in a rural café eating cake, drinking hot chocolate and chewing the fat?

Cycling is thick with myths and old wives' tales. Don't go too hard before Christmas. Only take on that hill in the New Year. Riding in the rain will sap your legs. I love these old tales, and I love the way they have been orally passed down through the generations.

And I love that feeling of going fast that only a bike can give you. Hammering along in a tight chain gang of riders, nearly setting off the speed cameras. Wind in your face, pulling at your jersey. Hedges blurring past. Looking around and seeing others suffering while you are feeling wonderful. It's sick in one way, but that's how confidence in sport works. No one said it was easy.

WHY WE CYCLE AS WE DO

ALISTAIR We are on our bikes every single day of the week, often for four hours.

We do a two-hour ride on Mondays. Why? Because we've always done our easy ride then. One day three years ago we decided to make it a bit longer, added on a loop, and that's stuck ever since. On Sundays we do our long ride. Guess what? Years ago, aged fifteen and thirteen or so, we used to meet Adam from Triangle Bikes for a long ride from his shop on a Sunday. We do our hardest ride on Thursday evenings because that's when a chain-gang group of cyclists from round our way goes out. Fridays are easy days because it used to be my busiest day at school, and because Saturdays have always been race days. It goes on.

We do long rides on Wednesday afternoons because that used to be my afternoon off school.

JONNY I have borrowed Al's routine, but it all makes sense for me. The Tuesday-night track session works because you could never work that hard on your own. It's the same with the Thursday night chain gang. You'd have to be an idiot to attempt to replicate that effort on your own.

The fact that Al's done it all before makes it easier for me. He might accuse me of copying him, but some of it is unavoidable. If he goes along the Meanwood Valley trail, why would I go through Headingley? A few years ago Alistair started going for a little run after that Thursday evening chain gang. I'd be left standing there like a lemon with the bikes. There'd be no question that I'd be allowed to join. It was made quite clear that my job was to guard the bikes. Eventually someone else who trained with us pointed out to Al that if he did the run in a nearby field, we could actually hide the bikes and all manage the run. Finally I was allowed to join in.

ALISTAIR The philosophy behind our training is simple. It came from me thinking: triathlon is an endurance sport, so therefore you need to do lots of training. It's not about how fast I can cycle, but how efficient I can be – how fresh I can feel when I jump off for the run. And you get efficient by doing lots of it.

We've been phenomenally lucky in some ways. The fact we grew up in West Yorkshire with all its hills meant that we've got away with doing lots of easy riding, and very little cycling on an indoor turbo trainer (a triangular stand and fly-wheel that turns your ordinary road bike into the equivalent of a stationary exercise bike), because those interval sessions are all automatically built in.

Our routine has evolved naturally. Before the Olympics in 2008, my Monday ride was still only forty minutes into university. Some other triathletes would tell me it was a waste of time, but because I'd always got my cycling miles in by cycling to school, it felt right to me.

Around the same time I went away to Australia to race hard and pick up ranking points, but I raced appallingly because I had a little hip injury. I came back with only six weeks to go before the Olympic qualifying race in Madrid and decided the only way I could possibly qualify would be by absolutely smashing it in training. That forces you to develop your routine because you start thinking, how can I work harder? Where can I squeeze in an extra session? That compelled me to put in extra riding, to swap an easy session for something far more demanding. It was the same when I was trying to get fit for the 2010 season. That mix of tradition and evolution explains almost everything I've done.

THE HARD YARDS

JONNY The cold is something of a theme for us, growing up and now training hard in Yorkshire. Even after twenty-two years of it I hate it with a passion, and it's never worse than when you're out on your bike.

When you train in warm weather, your recovery times are so much shorter; a four-hour ride in the sun takes so much less out of you than a four-hour ride in the British winter. When the weather turns, biking loses almost all its appeal.

From a purely physical point of view the hardest bike session we do is a chain-gang effort, where a group of you take turns going hard at the front. But that feels like racing. We'll meet at six thirty p.m., and there might be as many as seventy of us, hitting it hard for 30 kilometres out and 25 kilometres back before finally cooling down. It's such good fun that you don't notice how hard you're working. The cold? That's different. That's just long, slow torture.

There's nothing worse than being two hours' riding from home and thinking, my hands are freezing, my feet are freezing. There is always the option of doing a set indoors on the turbo trainer, but that's so dull you will do almost anything to avoid it. I've had rides when my hands have been so cold that I can't open the front door when I get home.

ALISTAIR I remember one infamous mountain-biking expedition to the top of Whernside mountain, during a northern triathlon camp.

We set off in the cold and wet, following a stream, which was fine until I overbalanced while standing next to it and fell in. I was soaking wet. Three hours further on we were caught in horizontal snow. It was awful – all the girls were crying, I was running with my bike because it was warmer, and when we got to the bottom of the mountain we still had four miles to do along a road. It was hell. Although we still raced it, of course.

JONNY A dry cold is fine – blue skies, sunshine. A wet cold is shocking. On those long, wet, cold winter rides I'll be counting off the minutes until I get home. 'Three minutes to that hill, four minutes up it, five minutes along the road . . .'

I'll be praying that someone will be in when I get home so that they can open the door. You knock, and nothing. Somehow you get your keys out of your back pocket, get them into your mouth, and then shuffle over to try to undo the lock with your mouth because it's the only thing that can still move almost normally.

I hate the ice on those winter rides more than anything else. Two winters ago I crashed on ice twice on the same ride. That ruins it because if you're riding along thinking, please don't fall off, please don't fall off, then you aren't riding fast enough.

When it's miserable, Alistair will get to the point of turning round, and I'll say, 'I'm sure we can go just a little bit further . . .'

ALISTAIR The worst sort of conditions are when it's two degrees and raining, because it's just about possible to ride, but it's extremely unpleasant. I'll get out and do a long ride in that if I can. If it's absolutely unrideable – snow everywhere, ice on the roads – I'll take the mountain bike out. If I can't even do that, I'll be philosophical about it. It's just not worth it; you train so hard the rest of the time that it's good not to get too caught up in obsessing over exact distances and mileage.

Jonny will come back after a ride that's been truncated and then climb on the turbo trainer to make up the missing mileage. I won't do that. When his pedal fell off with an hour of training left to do, he came back, fixed it and then went out again to add on the extra time. If it's the day for a three-hour ride, he has to do a three-hour ride, whereas if training's been going well, I won't mind so much. He finds sticking to a routine very relaxing.

THE SECRET OF TRIATHLON CYCLING

ALISTAIR People try to train for triathlon in different ways. For me the secret to it all is efficiency. You want to get through the swim as easily as you can, then through the bike with as little exertion as possible, and then that allows you to run very hard.

JONNY There's another way of explaining the philosophy behind our training. Imagine we are trying to carve the perfect marble statue. There are different sections to focus on – legs, head, arms. If you chip away carefully at all of them, the statue will take shape. Focus too much on one single area and the balance of the piece will go. Work too hard on a single area and you can chip away so much marble the statue breaks.

For biking, the efficiency element is critical because you want to get to the run as fresh as possible, but also in the best possible position.

Because of this, our riding is entirely different from that of dedicated road cyclists like Bradley Wiggins or Mark Cavendish. Cycling after a hard 1,500 metre swim is difficult. So too is hammering it for 40 kilometres on a tight urban course.

Our training reflects that. We have even once practised cycling straight off the swim by setting up bikes on turbo trainers by the side of the pool. In races we will swim with a relatively small leg kick to keep fresh for the pedalling ahead. We will make sure we don't run too fast through transition one for the same reason, and we will cycle with a fast cadence after the swim to ease our legs in, rather than grinding away in a high gear.

Both Alistair and I like to put in a big effort quite soon after the swim. We hope most of our rivals will be tired; we will be relatively fresh, and that means we can either split the race up or pile even more tiredness on our rivals.

During the bike leg you should always be doing something. Move forward if you're in a group. Drink regularly. Eat when you can – I will always take a gel after 20 kilometres. A key weapon is the ability to change pace – lift it out of corners, chase down a break, respond to a move.

The last few kilometres of the bike are critical. It can be like a sprint at the end of a Tour de France stage – lots of nerves, lots of shouting, lots of shoulders bumping. If you are even 20 metres down going into transition you will have to make it up on the first kilometre of the run. Having to run the first kilometre in 2 minutes 45 seconds rather than in 2 minutes 50 might not sound like much, but it makes a huge difference.

BIKE TECHNIQUE

ALISTAIR You can't be too prescriptive about bike riding – you will find your own style through hours and hours of riding, and different body shapes need different positions on bikes – if anyone else tried to copy Bradley Wiggins's shape they'd be in agony within twenty minutes. But there are certain basics to concentrate on. Your upper body should be still; don't waste energy throwing your shoulders and head around. Keep your elbows bent and loose, and don't grip the handlebars too tightly – you need to be able to absorb road buzz. Concentrate on pedalling in smooth circles, applying power constantly all the way through the pedal stroke rather than stamping down, and keep your soles roughly parallel to the ground. Your cadence – the number of pedal strokes you make with each foot per minute – is an individual thing, but on steady rides it should be around 90–100 revolutions per minute. Much slower and you'll be working your muscles too hard for the same result.

Coaches' Corner

ALISTAIR Have fun on your bike, even when you're training hard. We always do. And try to follow a few of these simple rules.

- The key to good triathlon cycling is time on a bike. The more riding you do, the more efficient you become, and the fresher you will be going into the run.
- Long rides are a must, so plan time for them. Make them social; cycle somewhere exciting or beautiful.
- Riding doesn't always have to appear to be pure training. Commuting is a great way to clock up extra hours without really trying.
- It's better for your training and fitness if you can manage five hours every week rather than ten hours one week and none at all the next.

A good training session doesn't always need to be done by numbers. While you're out on your bike, you can decide to go hard between alternate roundabouts, or opt to really hammer it up any hills. But here's one that should help you in races.

1. Warm up slowly. If you race on a time-trial bike, use it for this session, whether on road or turbo.
2. Do eight minutes at your racing pace, three minutes of easy spinning and then three minutes at faster than race pace. Rest for one minute, and then repeat until you have done this a total of five times.
3. Warm down well, by gradually decreasing both your cadence and your effort over ten minutes, until you are spinning a low gear very easily.

Brother on Brother

ALISTAIR

The critical factor in the relationship between Jonny and me is the difference in our ages. From that two-year head start, everything over the next twenty-two years has followed.

I was the boss, the instigator, the leader – whether it was in the garden, with our toys, or when we began to mess about on bikes and in pools. When we first went to school I was the one in charge, the one who had to deliver notes to his teacher when he wasn't well, the one who had to look after him on the way in.

I was probably the naughtier of the two of us. Jonny always toed the line. I was more the problem one, and I think I wound our parents up by questioning everything they said.

Mum and Dad weren't strict parents, but there was a clear expectation of certain standards – that we would work hard at school, that we would be polite. The usual punishment was being sent upstairs to tidy your room. I was more scared of my dad than of my mum. I could answer back to her, but Dad had a tone of voice that struck fear into you as soon as you heard it.

Jonny's big beef with me when we were growing up is one that will be familiar to all kids with older siblings: he only ever got things second-hand from me, whether it was toys, clothes or games. Perhaps he should have focused some of that anger on Mum when she went through a stage of dressing us in identical outfits. Like any brothers close in age and in everything they did, we absolutely hated looking the same. There are some brilliantly humiliating photos of the two of us from that period.

There were tit-for-tat arguments and the usual struggle for sibling supremacy. I had a train set I really loved, and there was no way I was going to let him play with that; he had the Scalextric, so he imposed the same rules.

When our youngest brother Ed was born, I was seven and Jonny was five. Because of the bigger age gap between Ed and me, Jonny was delighted to work out that he could enlist a new ally. The alliances were quite clear: Jonny and Ed united against me, the two younger ones against the older one.

Jonny was by no means the dominant partner in that relationship. When Ed was about two it became clear that he was never going to be physically subservient to his big brothers. We wanted to have some space where we could have our toys out without him wrecking them, so Mum and Dad put boards down in the attic and let us play up there. There was a ladder that hung down, and it looked impossible for Ed to climb, but within a couple of weeks he'd worked out how to do it.

Jonny and I did fight – not just your average wrestling, but proper throwing-punches stuff. Our grandparents used to look after us from time to time, and as the fists used to fly Grandma would bellow, 'You two stop playing roughy-toughy!'

It got more difficult when we started getting closer in terms of sporting ability. I couldn't care less how good Jonny was at school compared to me, but the sport really mattered. Jonny always says that he went briefly off sport around the age of eleven or twelve. He'll refer to it as his dossing years. Well – I was there, and I know the competition was still just as fierce as it always had been. Jonny was still training as hard as ever, but mentally he had started dreaming about being a footballer or fly-half rather than a swimmer or runner.

I wonder if our personalities have developed in opposition to each other. The big difference is that while triathlon is what I love doing – there is literally nothing else in the world I would rather do – I've never got that impression with Jonny. He does it, and he does it brilliantly; but the motivation I get from pure enjoyment is something he doesn't share; he is motivated by an obsession for doing everything right, and on time, and by the book. He has to be on time for sessions because that is what motivates him to do it, not because he desperately wants to do things.

To understand Jonny, you have to understand that he likes to get things out of the way. He derives great satisfaction from ticking tasks off his mental list. He will get to swimming sessions early so he can get it done as quickly as possible, whereas I will get into the pool, swim easy for a while, hang around at the end. He does enjoy the sport, but just as powerful is the feeling that he has a duty towards it, a sense that he should do it.

Jonny has always hated change, and that's what makes me wonder how he will cope when he takes over at the top. He's always been this way, even at school; when he got a new teacher it would genuinely upset him. Years ago, right at the start of his teens, he got a running top for Christmas that was about as basic a version of the Adidas stuff we now have as you can imagine – pretty much just mesh, with the words 'Fast Track' in graphics across the chest. He barely took it off all year. It's the same now – if he gets a new top that he likes, he'll wear it obsessively until it wears out.

I think the way we adapt to change is one of the biggest differences between the two of us: I can cope with our training schedule being disrupted by bad weather or a coaching change, yet he will find it upsetting. For me exercise is exercise – run if you can't bike, bike if you can't swim, mountain-bike if the roads are too icy. For Jonny it's more, 'Right, I did this last week, therefore I've got to do it this week.' He likes things to be a lot more structured, a lot more quantifiable. He doesn't like that mountain-bike idea because it's not quite the same, because it might not be so far, because on a road bike you know exactly how far you've gone.

His world, just as it did when we were kids, revolves almost entirely around sport. He still supports Leeds United and Leeds Rhinos, and when he plays computer games it's usually Football Manager. In other areas of life nothing he does quite matches up to his sporting exploits either; while he's got through his history degree at Leeds Uni and eventually finished his dissertation on Richard III, he doesn't read much, can't cook very well and has so little musical ability it's frightening. It worked, albeit to his detriment. Today, if you were to play him two different songs one after the other, he wouldn't be able to tell that they weren't the same tune. Back at Bradford Grammar, only two people in the entire year were banned from the school choir. He was one.

I know sometimes he misses having a normal life. Sometimes, like all professional athletes, he knows it would be great to just have an ordinary day, full of rest, full of freedom – being able to go off and explore somewhere, put his feet up. He misses playing football, and he'd love to play in a five-a-side team like our mates. He always enjoyed team sports for the fact that you weren't the sole one responsible for your performance.

Nor has he had much chance to develop many relationships. As an endurance athlete you don't tend to meet many girls with a compatible lifestyle. At school he was always running or swimming. He never caught the bus home from school, the usual place for things starting to happen, because he was on his bike. As a senior athlete you have to be selfish to succeed. Your life has to be entirely focused around you and your needs. So you need a partner who understands that you can't go out with them because you're training, you can't go away for romantic weekends. You're also always tired. You just want to go to bed.

The move away from our parents was a big thing for him. He moved into the house I bought in 2008, when he was approaching his nineteenth birthday, but he spent a lot of time at Mum and Dad's. Our housemate, Alec, and I nurtured the independent side of him, and tried to encourage him to become his own man. But in some ways he was trapped, because he was still living in someone else's house. He remained a kept man.

When I see him nervous before big races, I do still feel a sense of being his big brother, of wanting to help him. But that relationship is changing as we get older, and as our careers develop. These days he won't let me tell him what to do so much, although race situations can be different. The tension forces you together in some ways; rather than it feeling like me versus him in Leeds, it's two lads from Leeds taking on the world together. And I enjoy those moments. Those little pockets of pressure are when I feel closest to him.

Jonny would deny it to the core, but I think his entire life has been about trying to compete with me. Trying to get level with me, and then beat me. There was a time when he wasn't into triathlon for its own sake; he wanted it because I had it. I could see his thought process: 'Hey, Alistair can't have it if I can't have it . . .' That has been his goal.

Growing up, I thought he was always trying to beat me, so it was always me trying to not let him. In terms of our comparative abilities he's got closer, moved away, and now got closer again, but still he wants to beat me.

Has it helped me become the athlete I am? Having someone to go training with, the motivation from seeing him go out training, learning bits from seeing him do stuff – all that must have made a difference. But if Jonny hadn't been around, or if he'd had no interest in triathlon, it would definitely have had some effect on me but not a decisive one. I think I would still have got to where I am, but it would have been a slightly different route, or taken me slightly longer. The question is how he handles the step from being the underdog to being the main man. I don't believe that it's hard to beat people; if you have the physical skills, if you're fit enough, then you will prevail. But the psychological battle is different. Does he really believe he can beat me?

His racing abilities are phenomenal. He is the most consistent athlete out there. In his last thirty-odd races, he has finished on the podium every single time, and in triathlon that is completely unheard of.

I always felt there would come a point when our physical abilities would come together, when we would beat each other. In triathlon it is so hard for one individual to maintain the dominance over his rivals because there is such a large margin of error. You only have to be a fraction off in one discipline for it to have catastrophic effects on your overall finish. So if I have a bad day he should beat me; if he's a fraction off I should beat him. Where it gets interesting for me is what happens if we're both racing on our best days. Then who comes out on the top?

I like to tell myself that it's enormously tough on you mentally to compete as siblings, as we do. If you're the older sibling the pressure to stay ahead all the time is incredible. It can buckle a lot of people. And as a younger sibling the pressure to keep up is massively tough. At some point one of you will buckle, and often that means the weaker one will drop away completely, because suddenly the goal, the motivation, has been taken away.

You have to be very strong to deal with it. I've gone to races and people have said, 'It must be hard for you. You're the best in the world and everyone – everyone – wants to be beat you.' And I've been able to say to them, 'Throughout my entire life I've had my brother trying to beat me at everything I do.' It has been an enormously positive force.

If you have the ability to step back and see that competition as a good thing, as a wonderful way of spurring you on, then you can deal with it. If you can't get past the pressure, you'll begin to hate it. Step back from it, and you can take great strength from it. And remind yourself that you are competing over sport, not about which of you has food in your mouth.

Jonny was noticeably more highly strung in 2012. Almost every race he entered there would be some sort of soap opera. It will sound pernickety, but with Jonny it's the little things that wind me up. I'll get to the pool, and he'll have made sure he starts as early as possible so he can do as many lengths as possible before I've started. He'll get out on his bike first so he can say he's been riding for a few more minutes. When I was injured, he'd be doing lots of little extra bits of training. Jonny would deny this. He says that, in my eyes, he could do no right during that period. But that is the tension that injury creates. Friends become strangers. Brothers distrust.

There's always a fascinating point in any sport when two seasons overlap. Athletes realign their goals, gain motivation, change direction. The Olympics accentuated that even more. It brought everyone's thinking into sharper focus: can I train harder? What extra sessions can I do?

Jonny's subconscious approach was to improve lots of small things incrementally, and that made him even more intense than normal. He was more highly strung than I'd ever seen before.

In Olympic year, he became much less trusting of me.

I couldn't give him advice any more. His thought process became, 'Why is Alistair telling me this? What is he trying to do?' I would tell him, 'Jonny, I'm doing it to make you faster.' If he saw me change my training, for example by adding in an extra run, then he would do it a week later. It's as if he needed proof that my advice was for the right reasons.

I interpreted it as Jonny worrying. He is a natural worrier; he is also quite reserved, and a lot of the time doesn't vocalize his thoughts. He also analyses everything. So I would have to play on that – I would ask him to analyse why his own brother would possibly be trying to make him worse.

He projects his way of thinking on to others. It's how he rationalizes situations. If I'm late leaving the house for a training session, so that he is waiting in the car for me, it will seem like a disgrace to him because if he left late he would feel hugely disappointed in himself. The fact that I wouldn't care if he were late doesn't occur to him. He will also be fiercely competitive about each of our achievements at similar ages, and can't understand that I might not be. Perhaps all younger brothers are like this with older siblings. But when he once asked me, 'Have you ever seen a result of mine and wished I'd done worse?' I was genuinely shocked.

Pressure is having to do things you wouldn't ordinarily do. It can be positive, if it makes you do something more, if it makes you try that little bit harder. But it can push you too far. That is my fear with my brother: the pressure could push him too far.

JONNY

I still get stick about how much I used to follow Al around as a kid. I had little choice in it. He was the dominant brother. If he wanted to watch something on television, he would win. If I did something he didn't want to do, he'd frown and say, 'What are you doing that for?' It's the same today. If I were to decide to do an extra training run, the same question would come out. It's only in the last couple of years that I've been able to stand up to him. If we're at home and there's a football match on that I want to watch, I can now get away with it.

Alistair thinks I have become more suspicious of his advice in the last year. I don't agree. His injury before the Olympics did change things between us. I think it was hard for him because he was unable to train, and there was nothing he could do about it. It's true that I have always believed anything he told me about training. Maybe as I've got a little older I've thought about it a little more. But I've never thought that he's trying to trick me.

We've done very well to get on as well as we do for so long. Living in the same house, doing all the same training sessions, competing for the same gold medal. The Olympic year piles so much pressure on you. I had never experienced stress like it. You could see it at the races. If people failed to qualify for their national teams, that was it – they were gone, finished as elite triathletes.

We were lucky that we could get away from it all in Leeds. We could have tea in a fish and chip shop in Guiseley and not be bothered by anyone. But I would go to races, like the World Series event in San Diego, and see athletes so nervous in the days leading up to it that they were unable to ride their bikes. You could see the strength draining out of people.

One of the great advantages of having Alistair so close is that I can constantly see what the best triathlete in the world is doing. If he isn't getting too intense about things then it stops me getting too worked up. If my brother eats sticky toffee pudding and he's world number one, then so can I. If it's raining outside and he decides he is going to ride for only two hours as a consequence, it allows me not to get stressed about missing out on what I would otherwise think were crucial miles. He has shown me what it takes to be the best.

Alistair is a lot more confident in himself than I am. If he decides that it isn't necessary to do that extra training run, it holds me back too. If he wasn't there I would worry about missing it. I would almost certainly get too tense. But when you have the world champion sitting opposite you eating chips, it tends to calm you down.

I'm someone who has to do something as well as they possibly can if they're going to do it at all. With my dissertation I knew exactly what I needed to get for a 2:1 degree – 45 per cent. I ended up getting 68 per cent. In many ways, what was the point of that? A lot of my mates said they would read a few books and that would do. I just couldn't bring myself to do that. I don't know why.

It's a pain in the arse, because it means more work. It's even true if I'm playing Football Manager on the Xbox. I have to do that properly. Or if I clean my bike – it has to be perfect. Alistair's influence helps me keep a grip on that side of my personality.

In return, I don't try to get one over him by sneaking out for an extra ten-minute run when he's finished training. We work together.

He has taught me a lot about enjoying sport. He has shown me that top athletes don't need to be superheroes, or do superhero things to win world titles. You can be normal and still make the Olympics. He was the first one to break that barrier for me.

Here's another lesson he's taught me: training doesn't have to be painfully dull to work. Without him I would almost certainly have trained too much, got caught up in being obsessive about what I eat.

There were others who helped underline that attitude. At

school, on presentation nights, Mr Kingham would take us down to the sports pavilion. We'd play football on the grass outside and eat chips, and listen to stories about legendary runners from Bingley Harriers. This was from a teacher who had guided Richard Nerurkar, one of the best marathon runners in British athletics history. I'm sure some of the tales were exaggerated, but the emphasis was always on fun.

When I was sixteen there was no coach saying, 'You must ride for four hours today.' We would just meet at the roundabout near our house and head off. 'Right, lads – where are we going?' We never asked how far we were riding. We heard about a café somewhere miles away and headed off. This was the culture we were brought up in.

Living together has worked for us in practical ways too. When Alistair was racing in Madrid, trying to qualify for the last Olympics, he tore the rear hanger off his bike the night he was supposed to fly out. While he packed his bags, Dad and I spent hours in the garage, torches out, taking bits off all the other bikes so we could get his race bike working. Other triathletes might have travelled to Madrid two nights before, with two spare bikes, but we were still training in Yorkshire, mending the bikes ourselves.

What I found hard to comprehend was that something as routine to us as riding our bikes, swimming and running, could suddenly transport us to the Olympics. We thought nothing of it. The Olympics was so distant, because it was something we watched on TV. And with London being a home Olympics we knew it would be even stranger – we would be sitting at home, playing Call of Duty on the Xbox, two days before the biggest race of our lives. We could have gone to the pub on the night before.

Our relationship has evolved in the last year. I feel less like the little brother now. I stand up to him more. There are other people in the training group that Alistair has got closer to, and he has his girlfriend now. I'm sure part of it is that he doesn't want me around him all the time now I'm his biggest rival. We're both growing up, and you can't expect your relationship to remain unchanged. If it hadn't been for triathlon he would have gone to university in Cambridge and I would have gone to Durham, and we would be seeing each other only occasionally. There would be three hundred miles between us.

Now, with the way we live and train, we feel closest to each other around races. It's the pressure. I know Alistair better than anyone else in the world. I know when he's stressed. He knows when I'm stressed. He gets agitated, and suddenly I can't do anything right. He will take it out on me. When he was injured and his Achilles was hurting him on group runs, I would get the blame. So I will keep a little distance.

When I look back now on what Al was like when we were younger, certain small yet significant memories stick out.

He was different to the rest of our mates when he was watching sport. They were always cheering for the underdog; he always wanted the favourite to win. He would back them to the hilt, even though it set him apart from everyone else.

Then there was the thing about heroes. I loved some Leeds United players. I could barely believe what Paula Radcliffe and Haile Gebrselassie could do. Alistair enjoyed watching great cyclists, but he didn't have any heroes. In triathlon he's raced against the athletes he admired as he came through, and he's beaten them. Maybe he's just not very respectful sometimes. But I know that there have been a few that he's cycled past and thought: bloody hell, you are terrible at riding a bike. Or, you can't ride in a straight line. Or, you've got no idea about technique.

When the two of us get invited to big awards ceremonies or dinners there's usually only one thing on our minds: when's the food coming? Where's the bread? Classic endurance athlete behaviour. You're always hungry and you're always tired. But there was one dinner, when we were sitting near former Olympic Champion Adrian Moorhouse, that Alistair still remembers fondly. Moorhouse was asked by a rather pompous fellow guest why he bothered training for thirty-five hours a week. 'Seems like a complete waste of energy to me!' Adrian's answer made complete sense to my brother: 'If you can ask that question, you're in the wrong game.' So while he won't put anyone on a pedestal, he has taken little bits and pieces from people he admires.

Alistair is more stubborn than me, which has its advantages and disadvantages. He does what he wants to do, and he sticks to it. But he is a lot less stubborn than he was five years ago. He is a lot more likely to listen now and he is more open about what he is doing in training.

He is more settled than he was, and he has mellowed. He has also become better at losing. It won't destroy him as it used to. I learned several things early on: that you have to get on with things, that you have to do it yourself, that hard work pays off, and that losing, well, happens. I played more sports than Alistair when I was young – football, cricket, rugby. I failed at those regularly. I learned from that what I had missed, and I didn't want to fail again. And if you've made sacrifices like I did for triathlon – giving up the football and rugby – it makes you put in the hard work, because it has to be worth it.

One characteristic that remains is his appalling time-keeping. In that we couldn't be more different.

When we're catching planes he will insist on pushing it as far as he can. He likes to be the very last person on board. He'll wait and wait, arguing that this allows you to walk through and see where the free rows are for a kip, but it constantly causes problems. On one occasion, coming back from a big race, he really pushed it. We had some food, a drink, messed about, and we hadn't even been through security. We dashed through, pushing past everyone in security, shouting, 'I'm really sorry, our flight's leaving!' and then we got to the gate and those same people were on our flight. I had to hide in the corner.

Why rush if you don't have to? Why would I want to nail it to swimming and get my kit on really quickly? What's the point? I could go five minutes earlier, totally relaxed, but Al has to sprint to the car and get there at top speed. It's gone wrong for him many times, but he stays resolutely the same. He's missed rides, trains, even the wedding of our good mate Adam Nevins from Triangle Bikes.

On that occasion we were taking part in a fell race up in the Lakes on the morning of the ceremony. The pair of us had been chosen to do the first leg, and we were running along a ridge high above a scree slope. We were lost. Our solution? We plunged off over the side, slid down the scree and, obviously, then found we couldn't stop. Halfway down, the inevitable happened – he fell backwards, landed on his arm and shoulder and looked down to see an enormous gash with blood pulsing out. Trouble.

For the first time in my life I no longer gave a shit about a race. He had to try to climb down a cliff holding his arm above his head to stop it bleeding, and was then rushed to hospital. By the time we got out the wedding had already started. As the bride went up the aisle we were parked in a lay-by, getting changed into our suits as cars drove by, covered in mud, and in his case blood too.

I don't wish to paint a portrait of Alistair as some sort of uncaring hard nut. There is a side to him that would astonish people he's bellowed at in races or destroyed on bike rides.

Your first surprise: he won a singing scholarship at school. Your next: he once won a talent contest by singing 'Don't Cry for Me Argentina', although, sensibly, he's now rather keen on keeping that quiet. It's probably his most embarrassing moment of all time, not least because it's a song for a lady, but then again his voice was more Aled Jones than Tom Jones. Oh yes – and he played the flute, admittedly initially because my mum played it, but eventually so well that he got as far as grade six. His guilty pleasures? *Only Fools and Horses*, which is fine, and romantic comedies, which maybe aren't. The only two DVDs we had when we moved into his house were *Bridget Jones's Diary* and *Love Actually*.

Fashion? I cannot remember the last time either of us bought clothes. We get everything we need from Adidas. If we eked it out we could probably still be wearing sponsored clothing into our eighties, although it might look a little strange bowling round Leeds in GB tracksuits and racing-flats at the age of eighty-five.

What my brother misses most as an elite athlete is spontaneity. At the elite level there is a complete lack of it. He will admit that he is a selfish person, for the simple reason that he has to be totally focused on his sport. We live in a very strange world. We literally don't have the time that other people have to build normal relationships. 'Fancy doing something on Wednesday night?' 'Sorry, I'm riding my bike.' 'How about Tuesday?' 'Track session till late, then food and bed.'

Alistair doesn't always say much, so it can be hard to gauge when he is bothered about something. Is he upset, or does he just want to keep himself to himself? It's not always easy to judge. And, beyond that, if I were sympathetic, he wouldn't want me to get extra credit for being sympathetic. That's how fraternal relationships work.

There was one occasion when he got a new time-trial bike frame from Boardman Bikes. To him it was essential that he had this thing working. Housemate Alec and I spent the whole day getting it fixed up for him. Al was racing in the European cross-champs. He used the frame for a week and then decided he didn't like it, without really thanking me. I was gutted. But sometimes he doesn't show his appreciation for things like that, or say thank you. You know he does appreciate it, but he doesn't feel the need to say it.

Alistair has always been slightly parental towards me. So it may be that he resents the fact that I left home and moved in with him, which he sees as me not being as independent as him. He was twenty-one years old when he bought his own house and moved out. From my point of view it had taken him almost as long to leave home, and I'm sure it helped him having me move in with him.

At school he wouldn't want me to run with him. I think it was a little-brother thing. He had his running group and he didn't want anyone in there to slow him down. It was the same on the bike ride in. As soon as there was space on the canal tow-path he would accelerate away so he could drop me. If he deigned to stay with me he'd constantly complain that I wasn't riding fast enough. If I hadn't been there I'm sure he wouldn't have cycled anywhere near as fast.

We have learned not to make so much of the tiny goals within a goal. It's essential for our self-preservation. If we were competing over every single repetition in every single session, we would have killed each other years ago.

About two months before the Olympics I was asked what would happen if the two of us found that we were away on our

The sailor suits were Mum's idea. We're more grateful for the early swimming lessons.

We were always very competitive as kids. Look at the aggression from Alistair and the fear from Jonny. Shutting your eyes while stick-fighting is never a good idea.

We spent most of our childhoods outdoors. Al is taking over the map-reading, so we would shortly be lost.

Learning to sail on holiday in Spain – together, of course. A formative experience in the wearing of wetsuits.

ALISTAIR: Trying my hardest in one of Dave Woodhead's fell runs. I've just face-planted in a stinking bog. (Photo © David Brett)

JONNY: Leading out of a quarry on another of Dave's races. Rather pleased to be wearing number one. (Photo © David Brett)

JONNY: The baton on a Bunny Run is an egg. Here, we smash the baton. We still argue about whose fault it was. Alistair can't catch; I was school cricket captain. You decide. (Photo © Dave Woodhead)

ALISTAIR: Outside our grandma's cottage in the Yorkshire Dales, ready to climb the steepest hill we could find. Jonny loved that top almost as much as Leeds FC.

© Dave Woodhead

ALISTAIR: En route to winning the Auld Lang Syne fell race, proudly sporting the colours of Bingley Harriers. The prize? Enough chocolate to last a month.

JONNY: The school swim team shows off its trophy from winning the Bazuka National Relay Championships to Olympic champion (and old boy) Adrian Moorhouse. The first thing I ever won.

Team Kelme: Uncle Simon, Jonny, little brother Ed, Alistair and dad Keith. We liked to imagine we were in the Tour de France.

ALISTAIR: I was never happier than when running. Especially when I was about to win a fell race.

ALISTAIR: Hyde Park, 2010. I would collapse and know nothing about it; Jonny would make his big senior breakthrough, and the world would take serious notice.

JONNY: Budapest, 2010. I've just been crowned World Under-23 champion. It wasn't quite as easy as it might appear.

© Delly Carr

ALISTAIR: Winning the World Junior title in Lausanne, 2006. My first big win. Jonny crashed out on the first corner and ended in tears.

Leading the world in Madrid, 2011. Local favourite Javier Gomez is in the background. Shortly afterwards, the Spanish newspapers referred to us as 'the two gremlins'.

ALISTAIR: Breaking away from Bryukhankov and Gomez in Madrid, 2010. My first race back from a horrible stress fracture, and a result I could only dream of. (Photo © Nigel Farrow)

Topping the podium at the European Championships, Spain, 2011. Opening champagne bottles after a 1,500 metre swim, 40 kilometre bike and 10 kilometre run is harder than you'd think.

Training in the heat of Jeju before the 2011 Grand Final. Who would want chest hair in such conditions? Ironically, it was freezing during the race.

The Serpentine, Hyde Park, 7 August 2012. We swim hard; the biggest crowd triathlon has ever seen lends its almighty support. (Photo © Romilly Lockyer)

© Romilly Lockyer

The perfect team: Stuart Hayes leads us out. Stu was incredible. He buried himself for us.

JONNY: Somewhere between the end of the bike leg and the finish line, I would have to take a 15 second penalty. Exactly when I stopped, and how I dealt with it, would decide my Olympic fate.

(Photo © Romilly Lockyer)

ALISTAIR: Swim done, bike done. Half an hour of brutal running lies between me and Olympic gold. The moment of truth.

ALISTAIR: In moments like this, you have the strangest thoughts. 'Why can't I get this flag to open properly? Oh – I'm Olympic champion . . .'
(Photo © Romilly Lockyer)

JONNY: The support in Hyde Park was extraordinary. It was like running through a tunnel of noise. It actually hurt your ears.
(Photo © Romilly Lockyer)

© Romilly Lockyer

ALISTAIR: No words needed: legs gone, instead the hand bridges the divide between me and arch-rival Gomez.

© Romilly Lockyer

Brothers in arms: the finish line, Olympic triathlon, London, 2012. 'We've done it . . .'

Taking part in BBC TV's *Superstars* in the aftermath of London. It was supposed to be fun. We raced the 800 metres flat out. (Photo © IMG Media Ltd)

Catching up with another endurance expert. 'You ran that last 800 metres in *what* time? You two ran 10 kilometres in *that* time, after swimming and biking?' (Photo © IMG Media Ltd)

own on the run. As the younger brother, would I have the self-belief to try to hurt Al and the confidence to think I could actually win? At the time I thought I would struggle. Even to take it down a notch, would I make the first move or would I wait for him? I knew I would hesitate. I would never give up, but I would hesitate.

Around that same time we had been doing a track session. Alistair had a bad stomach, and I knew I could drop him at any point. If that situation had been reversed he wouldn't have thought about it at all – he would have just gone. Bang. But I was running round thinking: Alistair is struggling. He raced at the weekend; it's probably taken a lot out of him. I could drop him at any time – but he's my big brother and if I do he'll get in a mood . . .

It may even be a subconscious thing, that tiny element of submissiveness. He's the big brother. At the Inter-Counties in 2012 I was in good shape, heading for a possible medal. And with three kilometres to go the thought that crept into my head was: Alistair has never medalled at the Inter-Counties. It would kill him if I do. He will be at home with his leg in plaster desperately wanting to do what I'm doing.

It's always been that way. As a teenager I was running at the Northern Cross Country Championships. Alistair had taken silver a few times but never won. I was off the front with one other guy, and again the thought was there: my brother will be gutted if I win this.

In Olympic year there was another big factor at play: I had never beaten Alistair when we had both been fit. When I had come out on top they were both freak occurrences – I knew he was below par, I knew what he had gone through the week before. I didn't know how to beat him. But he knew how to beat me. And I felt that if I were on my best-ever day and he was on his best-ever day, then he would beat me.

It's not a fraternal blind spot. If I were to train with anyone who was constantly beating me in our run sessions, then I would assume they would beat me in a race situation. That's just what happens. When Alistair and I play each other at tennis, I have always won. So I expect to keep winning.

My early thoughts on tactics for the Olympics were thus relatively simple: race my best race. Not race to beat Alistair, or race to beat Gomez, but race for me. At the same time, for me to have my best race – and for Al to have his – we knew we needed each other – to push it hard on the swim, to push the bike. And what are the tactics when you know that if you swim faster, bike faster and run faster, you will win? You can try to surge, but ultimately it's how hard you can run that final 10 kilometres.

I did wonder what would happen if it came down to a sprint. I felt it would be close. I was pretty sure Alistair would try to push it a long way before that, because he would want to intimidate me with how easily he was running, and because he would know that I had the slightly better kick.

What will Alistair be like as and when his racing career comes to an end? What will he do with his life without the thing he loves most to hold it all together?

I know he would still want to be running and riding every day and I know he could never do anything that would require him to wear a suit. When our training is at its most intense I'm sure he would love to be able to ride to the café and go home without all the pressures of brutal sessions. To just enjoy the ride for what it is. But how long would that last? Maybe he needs the competitive element. He loves doing sport, but to do it to the level we do there's 10 per cent that isn't enjoyable – getting up so early in the morning, doing the hard sessions, training when you're tired, going out in the rain. The secret to a long and consistent career is to keep that percentage as small as possible. But maybe that 10 per cent is also what motivates you to do it all. If he were riding and being the fat one at the back of the group, would he stop enjoying it?

I often wonder if we'll be the sort of ex-sportsmen who are whippet-thin, or the sort who bloat out and become big fatties? I think I'll be okay. And Alistair will get fat.

Strange though it may seem, he puts on weight easily. He claims that's because he has only ever stopped exercising when forced to by injury. His appetite has never had the chance to adjust; he's just kept eating. When you go from seven hours of training a day to sitting around with a cast on your leg, you will put on weight.

He'd rather like to be an international man of mystery. Main residence in the Yorkshire Dales, with nice riding on the doorstep, but also with a place abroad, somewhere mountainous where he could ski and climb.

As we get older, we both appreciate warmer weather. It's tough training hard in cold, wet weather. I can see us in the south of Spain, clubbing together for a little house where we would each have just a few clothes and a bike, so when the weather gets really bad in the UK we could jump on a budget flight and be away from it all in just two hours.

To train as we do means each day, and each week, and each month must be very structured. You cannot be spontaneous. You cannot do anything outside your training plan. Some nights our friends will go go-karting, but you know that you can't because you have to be in bed early for your swimming session the next day. So much of your life is rigidly fixed. Neither of us would ever swap what we do. Not for the world. But that's what you miss.

Our routine was ingrained in us from the way we were brought up – from all those swimming lessons, all the outdoor activities. It was almost as if we knew nothing else. As early as I can remember we would get in from school and go off swimming; at weekends we would always be running and walking. Maybe we never knew what we were missing.

Inside a Race

ALISTAIR

There is nothing better than racing, and there is nothing better in racing than doing it at the very highest level. But the air at the top is thin, and the stresses on your body are immense.

It begins, for us, four days before the hooter goes.

This is the start of it: the taper, where you drop the volume and intensity of your training right down to leave you as fresh and fast as possible. That's the accepted theory throughout endurance sports. The reality can be a little more complicated.

Jonny finds that if he tapers too much – if he eases off the training a fraction too quickly, or too far – then his body can actually shut down. It's a little like the old thing that when you go on holiday you get ill; your body thinks it is time to rest, so it begins to drop out of competitive mode. He's been at races when he's gone out on his bike for a course recce with the British women, who will be racing the same course the day before us, and the girls will be dropping him.

There are other factors that feed into it. A day's travel by plane and car (and World Series events invariably involve this) makes your legs feel sluggish; if you're also racing somewhere warm (which, as we race in summer, we usually are), you'll feel lethargic too. Then, when you arrive in the host city, you spend your spare hours sitting around in a hotel, not doing much, eating and eating to load your energy reserves. Put all that together and your body suddenly feels slow and strange at the exact point that you want it to feel fast and fresh.

Now that I understand what can happen, I've played around with my approach quite a lot. It seemed to me that it was a much more high-risk strategy if I tapered significantly – while I could potentially get some really good performances out of it, I could get some really poor ones as well. I found that if I maintained my training routine, kept everything as standard as possible, and then eased off just a little bit, it was a lot safer. On any given training day you can perform pretty well if you're fit. It therefore seems logical that you don't need to ease off too much to perform at your peak.

Racing closes in on you in stages. With two days to go, we are called into the official briefing, and at a stroke grown men are transformed into naughty schoolboys.

No one wants to be the first into the room; no one wants to sit at the front. We deliberately arrive as late as possible and leave as early as we can. It's all something of a charade – it's always done in English, which means half the athletes there don't understand it, and a pompous official will talk at length about a course you will have raced five times before. They tell you about the weather, there'll be a big speech from some notional form of president, and then someone will ask a question that nobody else understands. All of the rest of us will then look daggers at the guy who's asked the question – 'Do you not know we want to get away?' Sometimes they'll lock the doors on you, and that's when you know they're going to drug-test you. When they don't, you queue up to get your race number and timing chip, but since no one wants to be on their feet in the queue, this becomes the first part of the race – who can get to the front of the queue the quickest? I like to sit there and wait it out.

JONNY

It's the first time you see all your rivals. For me it's the point when the race becomes real.

Athletes who train together tend to stick in the same groups. The Germans will hang out together. The Russians will have their own little corner. No one has their game face on yet. They're just busy trying not to limp, or trying to limp, depending on their mentality. You look around surreptitiously, wondering if so-and-so is looking fit, if that guy's in form.

The schedule is always set. At eight a.m. on the day before the race you are allowed to look at the swim course; at ten a.m. the bike route will be closed off so you can ride a recce.

The race itself won't start until two p.m. the next day. I will try to get up as late as I can. You want to sleep in, and you want to be thinking about the race as little as possible, but you don't sleep anywhere near as well as normal because you're nervous, or because you've tapered off your training so you're not as tired as usual. And then, for me, the nerves begin.

ALISTAIR

Triathletes being triathletes, a lot of the people we're racing can't get to seven thirty a.m. without doing some sort of exercise. We will be sitting in breakfast at nine o'clock – a big bowl of cereal, toast, scrambled egg – and out of the window we'll spot the guys coming back in from swims and runs. It never fails to amuse me – one of the best things about racing is that you don't have to do any training, so to behave as if you do is absolutely ridiculous.

What will have happened is that, at a triathlon in the distant past, someone will have gone for a run on the morning of competition and had a good race, so they have then decided to stick with that routine for evermore. At times, I've almost been sucked in – you wake up and think: hmm, maybe I should go out to test my legs. But you're far better saving your energy for the fierce exertions ahead.

JONNY

In the hotel on that final morning I'll be on my feet, unable to sit still, trying to think about anything but the race. Alistair and I will often share a room and we might try to watch a film, play a computer game or read a book, but I won't really be concentrating on them. Subconsciously I'll be thinking about the race.

The nervousness will manifest itself in strange ways. I like to pack my race bags really early, know it's all there, unpack and pack it again, make sure my shoes are the perfect tightness. Endless check and check again. Alistair could not be more different. The tasks that have taken me hours he will do in the five minutes before we leave.

When it ticks round to three hours until race time I will begin to feel waves of illogical panic. Will we get to the race on time? If we don't, how can I get my kit ready? How can I do my warm-up? I will have decided the previous night that I want to be down at the race by eleven thirty, so then that becomes the most important thing in the world, more important than the actual race. If I'm fractionally late – because Alistair is slow getting into the lift, which he often is – it'll be, oh no, this is a disaster, it'll be eleven thirty-five now. But I always get to the race and think, oh, I've got absolutely nothing to do now. Why was I rushing?

Alistair is able to be much more Zen about it. As long as he is physically fit he has never been that bothered by pre-race nerves. In the hotel he actually enjoys doing nothing for a change, sitting there reading a book. He's become very good at believing that by the time you get to that point you've done everything you can do. You've done all the training, all the hard yards, and you can't ask any more. All you can do is sit there and enjoy it. You can't change anything.

ALISTAIR

When I see Jonny getting all his bottles ready, arranging his race kit in neat piles, I never wind him up; I know he's on edge, so I give him some space. But if we ever fall out about anything in those final few minutes, it will be about time. Jonny will say, 'We've got to go NOW!' And I'll say, 'Why would you want to get up ten minutes before you have to, just to stand around by the side of a lake waiting for everyone else?' But Jonny just has to be there.

JONNY

Al will always abuse my nervousness. He knows I'll do anything to leave at a certain time. He knows I'll get his water bottles ready. I'll get his bike and run shoes out. He knows he can work that situation to his advantage.

Fifteen minutes before the race, even he has to start to concentrate. Athletes will attempt to get rid of their nerves in different ways – using stretch cords to warm up, loosening shoulders with big arm swings. Some are very chatty. You'll talk about absolutely anything. Suddenly even the least amusing comments are found to be hilarious. Everyone's laughing away, yet you know almost everyone is on edge. You can see it written on their faces.

My panic will be turning my stomach. I've forgotten my shoes. Something's happened to my bike in the transition area. Maybe I've forgotten the number of laps on the bike. I'm sure I haven't, but for some reason I have to check. Alistair will ask too, but he often genuinely doesn't know.

How bad do I feel? If you were to hand me a magic button that could spirit me out of there, just before the hooter goes for the first race of my season, and take me home to Yorkshire, I'd press it without a second thought.

Strange thoughts float in. Why am I doing this to myself? What would I be doing if I were at home? I could be on a nice café ride now.

I have to remind myself that I did all that training so I could be here: Jonny, enjoy it – you don't do all that training just to ride your bike – you do it so you can be here.

But oh, the worries can be relentless! What happens if I have a bad swim? What happens if I then miss the main group on the bike? The benign angel on my shoulder says, 'But you've never missed a break in your life. You've always been in the top five on the swim, why wouldn't you be now?' Then the devil pipes up again: 'What if you get beaten up, and you get dunked?' And the angel replies, 'It doesn't matter, you can get back up to them anyway.'

The irony is that, until the London Olympics, none of those worries had ever been realized. I've had bike crashes, because I've forgotten where a certain pothole is, but my bottles have never been in the wrong place, or my gels fallen off, or my helmet not been where it should be.

ALISTAIR

Without wanting to sound cruel or as if I'm gloating, all that hype and noise doesn't affect me quite as much. Managing that adrenaline is a key weapon for a top-class athlete, yet you see countless examples of racers being overloaded with it. That's why the Olympics can be such a minefield for so many people – all those normal nervous feelings are heightened and expanded. You need that adrenaline to be at your very best, yet you need to be the master of it.

The most significant worry for me is whether my legs will feel good. This is one of those nebulous, non-scientific sensations that really should be within your control, but very little about it makes logical sense. If the legs feel good you can do anything. You can control the race, you can sort everything out. If your legs don't feel good you've got no chance – and although this will sound bizarre, you'll often have no idea in advance how they'll feel when you ask them to respond. How they've been in the last few weeks, the last few days – none of it makes any difference. I've given up trying to reason with it. Some days I've felt absolutely exhausted the day before, and then felt amazing in the race; equally, on others, I've felt amazing in the warm-up and dreadful as soon as the race begins.

There has, traditionally, been one other regular fear, which as events would transpire at the Olympics is somewhat ironic. The race officials can dish out time penalties for various minor infractions – not putting your helmet in the box by your bike in transition two; false-starting; not clipping on your helmet before running off with your bike. If that happens the first thing you'll know about it is when you see your race number flash up on the screen, which is your signal to pull into a penalty box (triathlon's rough equivalent to a pit stop) for fifteen seconds at the start of one of the following laps. Again, it was an irrational fear, at least until the biggest race of our lives. The only time either of us had ever been hit with one before London was one year in Kitzbühel, when I was having a shocking race and so was actually quite glad of the rest.

Bizarrely, old injuries can be a help in those brief, scared moments before a race. When you've missed so much training and racing and experienced a powerful yearning to be able to do both, you are aware of an untouchable appreciation when you finally can. Back in 2008 I had quite a few niggles. When I felt fully fit at the European Championships, it gave me a wonderful buzz to be back in a racing environment and thinking only about the race.

JONNY

The way your body reacts to the stress of racing is genuinely bizarre. Quite often, pedalling slowly from our hotel down to the start, I can feel so heavy-legged that there's no way I can imagine being capable of going any faster. Yet it means nothing. You get to the race and you're absolutely fine. Why does it happen? The level of intensity at a big race is so far above everything else that your sensations can be knocked out of kilter, and riding to the race triggers entirely different feelings in you than the actual race does. I rationalize it as the lull before the storm. In the lull you feel devoid of energy, but you know there's a powerful storm coming that will carry you along with it.

As the seconds tick down, the oddness of it all increases. As I wait to be called on to the pontoon for the start, I'm usually swinging my arms about, which means my dominant thought is a simple one: does this make me look like a twat?

It's not ideal. There are serious decisions – race-changing decisions – that need to be made. The athletes line up in world-ranking order, one to sixty-six, and get called through on to the starting pontoon as their names are announced to the crowd. If you run on first, as the number-one ranked triathlete, you get to choose where on the pontoon you want to stand. By the time you're sixtieth you'll only have six spots left to choose from. But where is best?

One of the elite GB coaches might take us aside that morning and steer us towards a particular spot because it will be a slightly shorter distance to the all-important first buoy, but you'll often switch it even as you run on. Being first or second on can bring its own problems. You can be left standing on that pontoon for an age, waiting to go, waiting for all the other athletes to come on. Do you ignore all the fuss? Do you sit down? Do you talk to the official behind you? If you get called on eighth, that's almost worse, because you'll have three on the left-hand side of the world number one and four on his right. Now what's the best side? Sometimes you look up and think, oh no, *he's* next to me. You don't want to start next to someone who's a poor swimmer, because you can't work off them. They'll be drafting – slip-streaming – off you, which will slow you down. If someone's positioned just off your hips when you're swimming it makes it five or ten per cent harder for you. It feels as if someone is pulling you back. You can look up and think, please don't stand here, please don't stand here . . .

Portentous music plays over the PA, bass-heavy stuff designed to sound like an enormous heart beating. I try to focus on the practical – I must have a good dive, get a good first stroke in. To keep myself calm I try to remind myself that the race will take almost two hours. Therefore it doesn't matter how much I mess up in the first two seconds. I can always get over it. But one thought starts to push all the others away: let's get on with this.

ALISTAIR

Until you've raced at that level, it's impossible to understand the intensity. I have stood on that pontoon before huge races, trying to loosen up my arms by swinging them around, and I can barely lift them over my head. And then as soon as the hooter goes, you completely forget about it.

It's all about who you dive in next to. The ideal scenario is that you swim next to someone who's a bit faster than you, especially over the first lap, so they can tow you round. You get a fantastic drag effect if you just sit on their hips, as long as you're slightly behind them, although for the record if I have ever drafted off Jonny it's only happened once.

He hates the naughty stuff, and that means he cannot wait to get round that first buoy, because that's where the big fights go off – you get kicked, you get elbowed, you can get your goggles knocked off.

Everyone wants to take the shortest route to save time, but, perversely, you're often better taking an outside line, just to stay out of it. Get in the way and you can get pushed underwater – and if you go down, you're staying down. It's not spite, and it's not cheating; it's just a natural reaction if you're there to be grabbed. If you don't do it, someone will do it to you.

It was one of the big lessons I learned early in my career. We were racing the Hy-Vee in Des Moines, the richest race in America, and had just begun the bike leg when I heard someone shouting at me. I turned to my right to see the biggest bloke in triathlon giving me a terrifying look. 'Oi! I see you're wearing a black tri-suit. Somebody in a black tri-suit absolutely killed me round the first buoy.' I glanced back at him. 'Wasn't me . . .' 'That's good,' he said. 'Because I'm going to kill the bloke who did it. And I know he was British.' 'Oh,' I said, 'it must be Clarkey or Stu.' I turned away quickly before he saw my face. There was a very good chance it had been me.

Those early races were full of revelations. I used to think: okay, if no one touches me, I won't touch anyone else. I'll be nice. And then, after a few tastes of how it worked, I thought: to hell with it – if anyone comes anywhere near me, I'm going to absolutely kill them.

Sometimes those collisions can come down to luck; sometimes it can be your own fault. In the Olympic test event in Hyde Park in late summer 2011 we happened to choose completely the wrong side of the pontoon from which to start. When we dived in it was carnage. We fought our way to the first buoy, fought our way to the second buoy, then all the way down the back straight. For the best part of 800 metres we were fighting our way through. Normally by 400 metres we're pretty near the front. When it goes wrong, you just have to keep fighting.

For all our experience things will happen that make no sense. Jonny and I, without ever planning it, almost always bump into each other at the first buoy. We can start at opposite sides of the pontoon, but I'll glance to my left at the buoy and Jonny will be right there. It's amazing.

JONNY

My instinct is to avoid the madness if I can. I never swim over anyone on purpose. But you can't back off, because as soon as you do that you'll get dunked.

This lesson came from our junior races. You'd have a hundred and ten people all around you on pontoons designed for seventy. As you hit the water it was like a piranha feeding frenzy. At other times you weren't even allowed to dive in, so you had to start in open water. Mayhem. You wouldn't have one clean stroke. Bang – that's someone's head. Bang! There's another.

We learned from that, yet I've never liked it. Even now I will swim hard from the gun with dread about that first buoy filling my brain. It's indicative of my personality. I like to have everything controlled. If someone else beats you up you don't have that control.

Coming past the first buoy you want to be in the first ten to fifteen positions. You can swim past five or ten more on the next section, slot in somewhere near the front, and then the swim's easy for you. There is one simple rule: if you don't keep moving through the pack you'll soon find yourself at the back.

When it all settles down, when we're strung out in more of a line or elongated pack, the curious thing is that quite often you don't have a clue where you are in the field. I've had swims when I've thought: I'm having a terrible swim here, and then as I'm approaching the steps that take you out of the water at the end of the first lap I realize no one has got out, still no one's got out . . . and then I climb out and I'm second or third.

ALISTAIR

The tactics at this point are straightforward. I always try to keep moving past people until I can see the front, but I never actually want to be leading. Why? Because you don't gain anything from it – it can be easier swimming in the clear water, with your own stroke, but you're not going to break anyone at that stage. The ideal is that the leaders are in single file and you're third or fourth back, behind someone who isn't kicking too hard, and the person behind you isn't trying to swim past your hips.

If it's going well, and you're in that ideal third or fourth place, at this stage you can be thinking of anything – what you had for dinner last night, what you might do next week. Probably, because you're so relaxed, your brain almost switches off. If you're struggling or you're fighting someone, you're completely focused on the battle. Don't touch me. Don't come past me.

It's quite rare to find yourself thinking: this swim is hard. In a lot of races you're actually unaware of the effort you're putting in. It's instinct: I want to be at the front of the swim, I'll do whatever it takes to be there. In triathlon it's a great disadvantage to find yourself feeling: I don't want to go this hard this early in the race. It comes back to my philosophy of racing. I think of myself as a swimmer, a cyclist and a runner, rather than a triathlete. Swim hard, ride hard, run hard, and be capable of doing all three of those things.

JONNY

The sounds that filter through to you change with every lap and leg. You go from the hooter on the pontoon, which is so loud, to the beautiful silence of the swim. It can be so quiet that you can almost forget you're in a race. Then as you run out at the end of the first lap: a wall of noise, spectators shouting, dive back in, beautiful silence once again. In the water you can be in your own little world. It's the strangest feeling.

Once that first lap is done, me being me, I start worrying about transition one. Are my gels in the right place? Was there a flag near my bike? What colour was it?

Those irritating fears will continue to dog me throughout the race. Did I get off my bike behind the dismount line? Where is the dismount line? Come on, Jonny, of course you know where it is, you've cycled past it eight times on previous laps. Where does the run finish? Oh, I've run past it four times, of course I know. All these little things. Is my helmet set up right? Are my bottles the right way round? Eventually you have to tell yourself: stop. There's nothing you can do about it now.

ALISTAIR

Sometimes the adrenaline can make your own mind do strange things. In a race called the Iron Tour our bikes were racked adjacent to each other, and we were riding identical bikes. I came out of the swim just ahead, got to transition and, completely by accident, took the wrong bike. I was riding along a few metres in front, thinking, hmm, this seat is a bit low, and these shoes are a bit big, when Jonny chased up alongside me. 'You've nicked me bike, you big tit!'

JONNY

Alistair isn't as good at looking after his bike as I am. Every time I went over a bump on his bike the handlebars went down. I would never have raced like that because I would have checked everything. But then I wouldn't have taken his bike either.

The ups and downs of racing are strange. After the noise and excitement of transition, you jump on your bike, head out on to the courses and it's quiet again. No matter what sort of form you might be in, the first five kilometres always feel hard.

Sometimes the pace is so intense you can't even get your feet in your shoes when you want. I've had races, trying to catch Alistair, when my feet have been resting on top of my shoes for at least the first six kilometres. Eventually it quietens down and you can get yourself sorted. But you're trying to be alert the whole time for attacks. The pack moves so violently that it can feel as if you're in a washing machine. You have to think: go forward, go forward, go forward.

You need allies, and Alistair and I will always look around for each other. There is no logic in us both smashing it when we're ten metres apart. Wait for each other, work for each other.

There's the balance in your mental approach. You need to be alert, but you can't cross into being tense. You're on the bike for a long time, so you cannot be fully engaged for the entire duration. You need to find periods when you can relax. Repeat the mantra: whenever you're on the bike, always be doing something. So, if you're not working hard, be drinking. Constantly think about refuelling. I will always shout at Al to do it, and he will do the same to me. It can be dangerously easy to mess up. I've got to 30 kilometres before and suddenly thought, oh shit, I've drunk nothing. And that spells disaster.

Rational thought becomes difficult, because you'll be riding so hard, trying to stay smooth, covering all the breaks. Sometimes the course is so technically difficult, so twisty and narrow, that you don't want to take your hands off the bars.

You'll look around and try to work out what your rivals are going through. Is that guy over there looking tired? Then we need to make him work hard, or make it harder for him. That one over there looks knackered – right, we can forget about him. Him – he's looking strong, keep an eye on him.

Cycling brings its own unique type of physical pain. You kill yourself with effort at the front of the pack, go really hard over a hill, freewheel down the other side and then suddenly you're chatting again. It is also where the big arguments break out. 'Pull your turn on the front!' 'Do some bloody work!'

Racing in the World Series event in Madrid in 2011, Al, Javier Gomez and I were dragging the bike pack round. We were doing all the work. I looked back and saw Olympic Champion Jan Frodeno wasn't doing a thing. I was only twenty at the time, but laughably I wasn't having it. I dropped back. 'Come on, Frodo, you lazy git – come and do some work!' He looked at me desperately. 'Give me two minutes, two minutes.' 'No, Frodo, you can have one flipping minute!'

My personality totally changes in a race. I can go from being perfectly pleasant to brutally aggressive, shouting at anyone. The Jekyll and Hyde nature of it doesn't bother me; it's part of the race, and I'll do anything not to lose. I'm normally completely non-confrontational, and then the racer inside comes out.

I love these moments. It's the very heart of the race. And I particularly enjoy it when people are much more tired than you, when you're shouting at them to come through and then you realize, okay, you can't come through because you're spent. You look at them and think: you're suffering, and I'm not.

ALISTAIR

Cycling's the worst part of the race for me, because you take yourself to some dark places. You can become so mentally decrepit.

At the same time, I love being in the middle of it all. You see someone slagging someone else off, and your brain starts working out the tactics. Maybe it's because they're in great form and they want someone to work with them on a break. It might be because they're not feeling so good themselves, and the fear is making them panic. When you're rational and one of your rivals isn't, it's a wonderful feeling.

Our strategy remains simple: stay near the front. In that front five or so riders you're staying out of trouble; the chances of someone going down ahead of you and taking you down too are far less; there's also more room going round corners. If the first person to the corner brakes a little, the second person brakes a little more and the third person even more. If you're the fiftieth person going through, you have to sprint out of each corner to keep up.

You can also choose who you ride behind if you're near the front, and when some people are dodgier on a bike than others that can make a substantial difference in the final standings. If I ride behind Jonny it's pretty smooth; if he rides behind me it's the same. You have a good idea of each rider's skill set, and you make the calls accordingly. One rider will attack a lot but doesn't have any big kick, so you know you can jump straight on him. Reinaldo Colucci from Brazil tries to make a lot of breaks. Sven Riederer from Switzerland will try to do the same. You understand who the good guys are to follow.

I very rarely make attacks myself on the bike – it's more about being in a good position to cover other attacks – but there are so many different permutations. If the opportunity presents itself, I'll go for it. In Madrid in 2011, we came out of the swim in good shape. The bike course there is a really tough one, so we thought, right – let's keep this group of ten riders out front away from the rest of the field. And we also made it as hard as possible for the other eight riders in our lead group, including Gomez and Frodeno. Every time we came to a climb we would put the hammer down and make our rivals work their balls off to catch us up.

The two of us are now marked men, ever since we started

winning regularly. We have become the most watched men in the pack. If some random rider were to get out of the saddle and sprint away up the road, everyone would now look at us before doing anything, almost as if to say, what are those two going to do? If Jonny and I attack together, you can sometimes see our rivals thinking, ach, there's no point chasing them. I'm sure I've been away and people have thrown in the towel, so we now try to exploit that by doing it more and more.

Being brothers has an immense effect on how we race as individuals. If Jonny were in a breakaway, there is no way I would help chase it down. Jonny would never chase me either. Having said that, it does depend on how important the race is and how many people there are in the lead group. If there were eight riders away, meaning I had no chance whatsoever of a medal, then I would go after it. Jonny would ease off in that group and not do any work so it could all come back together. If it was two or three, I wouldn't chase because I'd know I could still come through for a medal.

I might also leave it as the prerogative of the others around me to chase. I've always got the excuse that I don't have to chase because Jonny is out front, and I'm not going to do anything to spoil his chances. Jonny too will watch and wait. If I'm out front and he's in the second group, he'll sit up and slow down, shrugging, saying, 'Well, I'm not chasing. My brother's out there.'

You use each other. Constantly. And as the Olympic qualifying race in London in 2011 illustrated, that is a weapon none of our rivals can match.

JONNY

The last few minutes on the bike can be cagey affairs. The race itself can feel as if it is flying past, but within that you have strange pockets of reflection. The big thing for me is wanting to be near the front when I'm coming into T2 – the second transition – because that will allow me to jump off my bike clear of the traffic and hectic mess all around.

It's imperative that you locate your station on your first attempt. If you go past it and have to run back, it's an absolute nightmare – not just in terms of time lost, but because you are now back among the flailing arms and legs, and because you have given your rivals a lovely free gift of the chance to get away from you on the run.

For the amount of time I spend worrying, it all happens so quickly. Once you're by your station, instinct takes over: helmet off, into the box, running shoes on. Suddenly I'm conscious that transition has gone. But it will always obsess me throughout the minutes that lead into it.

If you look at it rationally those fears shouldn't make sense. If I mess up pulling on my shoes it will cost me about a second. One second over a 10 kilometre run doesn't really matter. But as we sprint out of transition two, a palpable sense of relief will wash over me. Nothing serious can now really go wrong. My bike didn't break. I didn't crash. I didn't puncture. Now it's just up to me.

Into the run. Once again the atmosphere and sounds swirling around you change subtly. Now it's your own breath you can hear in your ears, the chat and banter and arguments between riders dying away.

There's a lot you can learn about your rivals without needing to talk. I know instantly when Alistair's feeling good. He likes to run at the front, but I can tell too from how he carries his arms, how he looks around, whether he smiles at a coach. He can tell how I am from my breathing pattern.

I can tell straight away how Gomez is feeling by what's

happening to his mouth. If his lips are pulled back, if his teeth are a little exposed, he's struggling. You can tell from where people run too. If they're tired they'll often run too close and bump into you. They're desperate not to get dropped, so they overcompensate.

ALISTAIR

We often hammer it out of second transition, but you can easily overdo it in that first kilometre. There's a difficult balance to be struck between going really hard and putting everyone else under stress, and not going full out. You have another nine kilometres to run. The race is seldom won in this first 1,000 metres, but it can certainly be lost.

Your brain is awash with stress hormones, and it's horribly easy to be overwhelmed by the moment and the chemical release. There's so much adrenaline and so many endorphins going through you that it can be a battle to remain in control of them rather than being swept away. Soon enough, however, there is just one physical sensation that begins to dominate all others: pain. And with every stride that you take, the feeling gets worse.

JONNY

The point of maximum pain hits you just around 8 kilometres. Why then? Because you've still got enough distance left that the end isn't in sight, and because you're thinking: I just can't go on like this for another 2 kilometres. You'd think it would get easier with experience, but I'm not sure it actually does. It stays hard, and you forget how hard it was last time. Only when you start racing again at the beginning of each new season do you suddenly remember how much it hurts.

It's almost impossible to recall that level of pain accurately, but I do know that there are different types of pain. There's that pain you feel at 8 kilometres when you're having a cracking race, when it can hurt as much as it likes and you'll actually quite enjoy it. That equates to the pain on the track when you're lapping in great times. The worst pain? That's when it really hurts, and you know you're racing really badly too. The same terrible thought plays on a loop round your brain: I'm hurting. I'm losing. I'm hurting. I'm losing.

ALISTAIR

The point in the run when you start to relax depends on who you're racing against. Sometimes, as with some of the battles I've had with Gomez, it's pain until the finish line. At other times you know from a lap out that you're feeling good and you know that you've won. And then you can enjoy it.

Once that lead is established you know whether it's in the bag or not. If it is, you can begin the celebrations from as far out as you dare. Being the person I am, I'd start the high-fiving and flag-waving and strolling and smiling from a lap out if I could. I've high-fived my way through an entire final kilometre before, although such chances are rare.

JONNY

I will never relax. At the World Under-23 Championships I had a lead of one minute with one lap to go. I began adding it up in my head – it's 2.5 kilometres, 60 seconds ahead, so I can only be caught if I lose more than 25 seconds a kilometre. That won't happen. But what if it does? What happens if I blow up?

I can't enjoy it until the last 50 metres. And even then I like to get through the finish line as quickly as possible. I can't do the dicking about – high-fiving spectators, grabbing Union flags, waving to everyone – until I'm right there.

The strangest thing about crossing the finish line is that suddenly everything in your body that has powered you along at flat-out pace for almost two hours suddenly stops dead. You lie there, legs gone, and think, if the finish line was just one metre further on, I'd never have made it. It's entirely a psychological thing, of course. If someone moved that finish line three metres on from where it should be, you'd still have made it. And the organizers hate it if you lie down, because apparently it looks less than glorious on television. They'll try to drag you to your feet if you're on the deck. But your body just shuts down.

ALISTAIR

I've said some awful things to race officials at that point – sworn at them, shoved them away. Some poor guy will be trying to take the timing chip off your ankle, and you're giving them a mouthful of abuse. That's what the exhaustion and elation do to you.

I've been asked why I will jog through the line when I could have continued hard and clocked a slightly quicker time. It's a no-brainer: because triathlon at the top level is all about your finishing position. Some rivals will say afterwards, 'Oh, I ran the second-fastest run split.' Who cares? It means nothing. Courses are often inaccurate. It's only the finishing position that matters. I might have walked the last 100 metres.

Something about triathlon makes people want to take

something away from every race. It's a sport of optimists. You can look down the results and find a meaningless trophy – third-fastest swim, fastest second lap on bike. Jonny and I have fallen into that trap in the past. You have to be honest. Is the run split really more important than the race result? I'd happily get the slowest run of the day as long as I won the actual race.

JONNY

Walking away afterwards, pushing your bike, hair sticking up with sweat, the fragments of other athletes' justifications and rationalizations can be both amusing and infuriating. 'Oh, I came twelfth, but I did the fastest run.' 'If only I'd made that lead group on the swim I'd have won.'

It's nothing but self-deception. Al will have killed himself on the bike to establish his winning lead. If that deluded guy does make the lead swim-group next time, he probably still won't win, because that harder swim/bike will take its toll.

Let's assume he can. The race is still not his. There are some triathletes who can only run after a very easy bike; some who will run exactly the same if it's a really hard bike or a really easy one; some who actually run better off a hard bike. So boasting that one small error in pacing on the swim cost you your chance is nonsensical.

It's the curse of triathlon. You don't get triple jumpers saying in defeat, 'Yes, I finished eighth, but my step phase was the longest. Praise me!' Yet I'm not complaining. We can use that curse to our advantage in races. If we know certain rivals are really looking at fastest run or swim splits – even if it's not consciously – rather than focusing solely on overall victory, as they should be, we can use that information to work out that we should really stretch them out on the bike leg. Tactics, knowledge, speed. That's the edge.

ALISTAIR

This may be considered a surprising and even depressing insight, but it's true: winning never feels as good as it should.

I've often asked myself why that is, and I think it's in part because you build it up and build it up so much before a race that no reality can ever match it. You can get so caught up in doing it doing it doing it, and when you achieve it it's too easy to be blasé about it. But – and this is the all-important condition – years of straining for the peak teach you a great deal. Through winning races, through going through brutal training, through having injuries – through all those contrasting experiences, you learn to appreciate it.

When I first started winning big World Series races it all happened so easily that I was initially rather nonchalant about it. Not any more. The injuries have shown me the other side of it. You win big races, go back to training and when it gets tough, when training is going badly, you remember that feeling, you remember that you'll really appreciate all this hard work.

Yet still, when you trudge back into your hotel room after a big race win, you close the door, look around and think: absolutely nothing has changed here. I might be sweatier, I might have champagne on my shoulders, but fundamentally I'm just knackered. You sit down on your bed, you have a shower. Your cuts hurt from where your tri-suit has rubbed, and your shoes have given you blisters. You're the same person you were before, but you're now hurting. That's hardly the cause for wild celebrations.

Slowly you come out of that dip. You sleep for an hour, go

down to get some food, and then the sane thoughts arrive: I've just had a great race. I'm a world champion. I raced the best and came out on top. But even in these moments it's not completely clear to me why.

Friends say that if they speak to me on the phone straight after a big win there's a calmness, there's a sense of ease. Another lesson from experience: now, at the ripe old age of twenty-four, I get over defeat and disappointment faster than I used to. I'll obsess over it for a day, but you have to clear it out. It's not that I'm happy losing; but these things happen. We will all have bad races. You can be frustrated, but you should never hate the sport nor what it does to you.

In those two hours immediately after a race you're in bits. But it's a great knackered feeling. It's a big part of what I do it for, that sense of being shattered, slightly dizzy from the champagne, but utterly satisfied.

The real dip comes a few days afterwards when I'm back in my training group, when you look around and think, nothing here has changed at all. After the big Hyde Park Olympic qualifying race in London in 2011, I really struggled for a couple of weeks. Qualifying for the Olympics was always my primary aim that year. So you race, win the whole thing, exceed your expectations and then feel like you can't care about anything else. And then you realize, hang on, I've still got the World Championships to come, and then the Olympics themselves.

I've always believed that if you do well then you should celebrate doing well, however you want to do it. When I first started winning races I thought I should celebrate every time I won a race, and celebrating then meant going out and getting drunk. When you start winning a fair few races you can't do that all the time. But you can still have a good crack at it.

RUN

WHY RUN?

JONNY There is nothing as pure and as simple as running, and that is where its joy lies.

What do you need but shoes? Wherever you are in the world, whatever time of day it is, however you are feeling, you can always run. Shoes on, door open, away you go. You can go anywhere you choose – across muddy fields, through city streets, along coastal paths and up and down hills.

It is a sport soaked in British tradition, from the middle-distance heroes of the past to the long-distance marvels and local club runners and legends of the fells. Through the simple act of running and competing hard you are joining that great lineage. And it is a sport that rewards everything you put into it. Train hard and you will get fitter. Put in the effort and the reward will come.

WHY WE RUN AS WE DO

ALISTAIR You might imagine that our training schedule is the result of thousands of hours of input from sports scientists, laboratory tests and many years of research from coaches around the world. What else could take you to the top of an Olympic podium?

Here's what else.

I do a long run on Monday mornings because at school I used to have a double free period on Monday mornings, and that allowed time for a long run. One of the critical pivots for us was happening to go to a school where you were actively encouraged to run. Running was freedom. Running was escaping. But I always wanted to get back for lunch, so the run was always about eighty minutes, and that's what I still do. And since I do it, Jonny copies it, and so it remains the basis of our run training today.

The track session on a Tuesday night? Same thinking. Years ago I told my dad I'd like to do some track work; he found a club and a session and it happened that our current run coach, Malcolm Brown, was there. Ever since then, Tuesday has meant track. And running on a Wednesday morning comes from me wanting to meet my friend Alec for a run around Meanwood in Leeds. I used to throw stones at his window to wake him up.

We will run every day, sometimes twice, for as little as thirty-five minutes to recover or as long as two hours to build endurance.

Thrown into this seemingly random mix is a fair amount

of trial and error too. We've tried things that haven't worked and then ditched them. Gym used to happen after a track session on a Tuesday, but that clearly wasn't working – we were knackered – so we changed it to a Monday.

All these things came together and created, almost by accident, the perfect training environment for two budding triathletes.

JONNY What sets us apart? I'm not certain everyone builds in the intensity that we have. A lot of our sessions are significantly shorter and faster than those of our rivals. As an example, when we were on our warm-weather training camp in Lanzarote in the winter of 2011, we were running 400 metre laps in 64 seconds. Some triathletes watching couldn't understand it, because our pace during races is closer to 71 seconds for 400 metres. What that intensity gives us is the ability to react to moves in races, and to make them. If you want to run 10 kilometres in 30 minutes, it's not just about being able to run a kilometre in three minutes – you need to be capable of running it in 2 minutes 50 seconds too, because the pace will rise and fall during the race itself. And if you are used to running faster, then running at the steady pace becomes easier and more efficient.

THE HARD YARDS

ALISTAIR Of our three disciplines, I'd say running gives you the most intense sensation of pain.

On the bike it's different – you can be in all sorts of bother and yet recover and be able to do it again. On long rides sometimes you'll hit a steep hill, you're only just able to get up it, barely turning the pedals over, and you think that you're at your limit, then you find you can do it all over again a few minutes later. You don't get just a second wind – you can get a third wind, and a fourth wind. Swimming gives you a more cardio-vascular pain. You might be doing 20 lots of 100 metres, and each one will leave your lungs bursting, but there's no impact, and there's less lactic acid. But when you're running, once you go really deep into your legs, you can't go that hard again. It's game over.

JONNY Of all our running sessions, it's the Saturday morning sessions that are the most brutal.

No matter how fit you are, you know you have to hit it as hard as you can. If we're doing a track session our coach might tell us to do 6 lots of 800 metres at 2 minute 16 seconds pace, and if you're feeling good then that pace can occasionally feel easy.

Not Saturdays. We run round a field. You have no idea

what might be on the menu, and it's all about time – six lots of five minutes, hard. You could be running faster than Haile Gebrselassie, but you wouldn't know about it. The timing of it is hard too. We start at nine thirty a.m., so that's our morning to sleep in as long as possible, and you'll wake up as late as you can to get that recovery in. But that has the downside of meaning you're not awake enough to fight the pain that's about to be unleashed.

There are different types of pain. There's the pain when you're running hard but making the times you've been set, and that's a nice pain. And then there's the pain when you're not hitting the times you should be, and you feel awful.

You're still working really hard with the nice pain, but the knowledge that you're somehow succeeding just carries you through. It's the same in a race. If you're coming through the pack and into the lead, the same level of exertion feels so much easier than if you're being overtaken.

THE SECRET OF TRIATHLON RUNNING

JONNY To win triathlons, you have to be a brilliant runner. That may sound obvious, but it wasn't always the case. Look at the performances that have won Olympic gold since the sport's debut in Sydney in 2000. Canada's Simon Whitfield clocked 31 minutes for gold back then; even Athens was won in 32 minutes. Now you have to be running sub-30 minutes for the 10 kilometres. And there's a big difference in those two minutes; sub-30 minutes for 10 kilometres is quick running. The majority of runners who are capable of that will just be running. They'll be putting in 60–70 miles a week, while triathletes don't have the space for that with the demands of the bike and swim.

How do you do it? With a fast cadence, and by keeping your upper body relaxed. You must be capable of coming out of transition two at real pace; in London, I felt as if I were doing a 100 metre sprint, and I'm not certain I could have run the first 200 metres any faster had the entire race been 200 metres long.

You must be tactically aware. As the run starts to settle down, usually about 2 kilometres into the 10 kilometre course, the jostling for position will intensify. A lot of runners don't want to sit at the front as it's harder than sitting on someone's heels, where you're in the shelter of their slipstream. But they will want to have the lead going round corners, so they can run the shortest distance and control the pace in and out. Al will always want to be out front. From there he can control it. From there he can dictate.

ALISTAIR Biking takes it out of your legs. Therefore, the first key factor in becoming a great triathlon runner is to have the ability to deal with that. You need to be able not only to run 10 kilometres very fast, but to run them very fast when you are tired and heavy-legged. Imagine how the last 10 kilometres of a marathon might feel, and you have some idea how hard it is to run fast in the last third of a triathlon.

You need to put in big mileage. And you need to be as efficient as possible. Your repetitions on the track enable you to run above race pace, and running above race pace makes it easier to run at that slower pace. If you need to win races with surges, you need that extra pace in your locker. You can get fit by training for 10 kilometres at race pace. But you will not be able to respond to moves, or make decisive moves yourself.

Very few of the 10 kilometres we run as part of a triathlon are even-paced. The first kilometre will always be very fast, and the second won't be much slower. The pace will then drop, before picking up again towards the finale. You need to be capable of dealing with those surges, of going hard if Gomez winds it up, of making a break in the final two kilometres after an hour and forty minutes of brutal racing.

Coaches' Corner

ALISTAIR The run is where you can win or lose your race. You'll be tired, but everyone else will be too. These little tips should lead to big improvements.

- As with cycling, the key is the time you spend training. You need to be as efficient as possible, so you can generate more pace with less energy and effort.
- If you are running three times a week, make one a long one, one short and the third a session where you build in speed or intensity.
- Triathletes often argue about how hard and fast running sessions should be. Personally I'm convinced that training faster than race pace is crucial. In training I never actually run at race pace.

This simple session is ideal if you have access to a track.

1. Warm up with a 5 minute jog, some strides and some drills.
2. Run 800 metres 10–15 seconds a lap faster than your race pace, gently jog 200 metres and repeat

a further five times. If you're just starting out, build slowly – start with 400 metres, then 600.

3. For a 40 minute 10 kilometre runner, race pace is around 96 seconds per 400 metre lap, so you should be aiming for 82–86 seconds per lap during your reps. Work out your race pace and train according to it.
4. Gradually warm down with a 10 minute jog.

If you don't have access to a track, you can do the session on road or trail by doing 8 lots of 90 seconds hard and 90 seconds easy.

Alternate this session with a longer interval session, like 3 lots of 10 minutes hard, or 5 lots of 6 minutes hard, with two minutes of easy running between each effort.

Remember that your hard and easy will not be the same as ours, or your mate's – know your level, listen to your body and train accordingly.

Here Comes Trouble

ALISTAIR

When clocks across Britain struck midnight on 31 December 2011, signalling the start of Olympic year, the country's attitude towards its elite sportsmen seemed to change gear.

Something clicked in the national consciousness: these London Olympics were real, and they were closing in fast. We had always been able to wander round Leeds without anyone batting an eyelid. I'd never previously been recognized by anyone who wasn't really into triathlon. That was all about to change.

We noticed it first when we were out on our long rides, or stopping off in cafés at places like Burnsall for our usual toasted teacakes two hours in. 'Are you those triathlon lads?' 'Are you off to the Olympics?' When you got home you'd glance at your BlackBerry and see Tweets from people who had spotted you – 'Saw you on the road to Blubberhouses' – 'Nice riding at Bolton Abbey'. In the context of sporting fame I'm aware it doesn't sound very impressive, but you have to put it in the context of our previous total anonymity. Even out running we would have passers-by shouting at us: 'Good luck, boys!'

There were other random factors at play, not least the insane growth of triathlon as a sport. Ten years ago, if you said you were a triathlete, most people didn't know what you did. Now most people at least know someone who's done one, if they haven't done one themselves. Then there was our sponsorship from BT, which meant the two of us were on the front of all

Yorkshire phone books in 2012. 'That's those phone book lads' you heard people say, or they would tap you on the elbow and ask, 'Could you sign me phone book, please?'

I tried to downplay the national excitement to convince myself that the Olympics were not such a massive thing. I've never been able to look more than a few weeks ahead anyway, so it was much easier for me to think about getting to the end of the particular training session I was doing. Yet there was equally no way of getting away from it; we both knew it was a huge deal, and in lots of ways it was going to change our lives for ever.

JONNY

We were used to a certain notoriety in our home village of Bramhope. It's not a big place, and so we know everyone. The woman in the local bakery is probably our biggest fan. She seems to know exactly what I'm doing at any time. 'Oh, you're off to Club La Santa in a week's time, aren't you?'

From January the interest just kept ramping up, even if the public seemed to think we were doing only one race. I was asked if it would get boring training all summer with no races until August. The fact that I'd have at least five other big races completely passed people by. The other misconception was the belief that everyone who does a particular sport well competes at an Olympics. The notion that you have to qualify didn't seem to occur to some.

Equally, all that attention made us realize quite how big the Olympics would be. People who had never previously cared about triathlon, or us, were suddenly keen to become experts. The guy in the corner shop would ask you. The postman would ask you. It was always there.

I couldn't wait to get my first race out of the way in San Diego in May. Until then it sometimes felt like there was a block of training and waiting, waiting and training, that seemed endless.

ALISTAIR

I was aware of the pressure that was being placed on us as potential medallists, but ironically only because people kept asking me about it. A reporter would say, 'Do you feel under pressure, Alistair?' and I'd think, well, I do now.

Public expectations don't need to be a burden. I was more concerned with the opinions of people who know me and my training most intimately. The public, while it's great to have their support, know very little about me and my form. My coaches, my family, my friends – they know about me, and I care what they think. I don't need to worry about what the public might expect.

You don't feel under more pressure because you're on a television advert or the front of the local BT phone book. But the fact that you're on an advert means you're recognized by that many more people, and they all talk to you; then the days you have to spend with your sponsors mean that you do more interviews and get asked more about pressure. It can escalate and escalate.

That balance between training and commercial work in Olympic year was one that would trouble many of Britain's Olympians, particularly those from sports which traditionally had a lower profile.

You get different sorts of athletes. For some, the training is what you do and the commercial stuff is part of the job. You don't really want to do it, but you know you have to because it makes you a living. For other athletes the commercial stuff is what they want to do, and the training is part of the job. They love the photo shoots.

We're both in the first category. We hate photo shoots. We'd rather spend as little time in a studio and as much time training as we possibly can. You can enjoy some of it – the chance to do something different to your normal life – but the days when you have to sit there having your photo taken, or make conversation with people you don't want to make conversation with, we could both find difficult.

There's a footpath at the Chevin Hotel in Otley, where we would fulfil lots of our media and commercial obligations, that has a great vista over the fields and hills. It became a favourite with TV crews and photographers. In Olympic year we jogged slowly along that footpath, up and down, up and down, for hour after hour. I'm not complaining; our agent is very good at scheduling in those commitments, and he has turned down big deals because they would involve another five days away from training.

But we loved the day-to-day preparations for London, the long rides and runs, the chain gangs and track sessions. We had always wanted to be elite athletes, not models. Why would anyone want a photo of our ugly mugs?

Some of the questions and opinions we heard in media interviews were surreal. Some people told me that I didn't want to be the reigning World Champion going into the Olympics; they told me it would bring too much pressure. They told me too that it would be a hindrance that Jonny and I had enjoyed such a dominant year in 2011, when, if I didn't win, then Jonny would.

I didn't believe any of that for a second. Would I rather be the best in the world or the second best in the world, wondering how the hell I was going to catch the champion? The logic is simple. The converse isn't. Would you rather be not-World Champion than not-Olympic Champion? It doesn't make any sense.

JONNY

There was another big change that we had noticed, and it came from those closest to us, those who would have the biggest say in whether we could win those Olympic medals: our rivals.

At the World Series race in London in 2011, Alistair went away on the bike. I got the sense that lots of others let him go, as if they felt they had no chance of beating him anyway. It was as if he was in a different race. In the two years from 2009 to 2011, Al went from being a skinny kid no one cared about to being totally dominant, to being the most feared athlete on the scene.

ALISTAIR

It all started to change for me around the Olympics in 2008. In a race in Des Moines, Iowa, I tried to get off the front on the bike, got caught and couldn't understand why I'd been chased down. One of the guys next to me shrugged and said, 'Because we know who you are now.' That was the point.

People tried to make it appear as if they weren't treating me differently, because they didn't want to give me an edge. But they were – there was a wariness in how they looked at me, an attitude when I was warming up. I became really aware that people expected me to win. They were looking at me all the time, and it didn't seem to matter who they were – if they were Javier Gomez, who might come second, or someone who might come in 50th. When I was in their shoes that wouldn't have made sense to me – when I was finishing 15th, then I was racing against the guys in 13th, 14th and 16th place, not the bloke in first.

It took some getting used to, but I tried to enjoy it. Think about it: it's a massive compliment, it gives you control over other people's strategies. When you see people spot you at a race, drop their shoulders and say, 'Oh no . . .' you know you're in shape, and you know you're in charge.

I've never understood the illogical confidence some people have, finishing 40th one week and being convinced they'll be 10th the next. Some athletes will make big statements on Twitter about what they're going to do, as if that will help them achieve it. There seems to be the idea that if people say it then it must be true.

Billie Jean King once said pressure is a privilege, and I think she's right. We both tried to stay the way we always had been; we trained with the same people, we hung out as part of the British team.

Sometimes, however, fate thrusts a stick through your spokes just when you least expect it. Little did I realize, as January became February, but my own optimism, my own world, was about to be shaken to its foundations.

As winter rattled past my confidence was high; the winter had probably been the best winter of training I'd ever had. When the Achilles in my left heel first began to ache I thought little of it. When you train as hard as we do, you ache all the time. But this was a pain that failed to fade with massage. Instead, with every run and ride, the agony increased.

I was sent for a scan. Nothing came up. They sent me for another. Nothing. Only on the third did they spot it, and the diagnosis was awful, the stuff of Olympic nightmares: I had a tear in the Achilles.

What made it stranger was that it was a vertical tear, which is so rare it was almost laughable. No one could tell me how I could possibly have done it, only that I had no option but to be clamped into a surgical boot.

Initially there was panic. How serious is this? How long will I be out for? Can I still get fit for London?

In the past I've pretty much stopped when I've been injured. Right, there's no point in me doing anything here – let's wait till the injury is fixed and then crack on. This time it was different. The Olympics changed everything. More than ever before I knew that I had to do everything I possibly could, to keep myself sane as much as for any physiological benefit.

The problem was that the only stuff I could do was stuff that felt pointless. In that first fortnight I couldn't do a thing. I had to keep the foot completely immobile to give it the best possible chance to heal, because any slight movement would have risked re-opening the tear.

When I could begin to train, very little and very gently, the work I could do still felt meaningless. There was always the suspicion that it was a complete waste of time – going on the turbo trainer and pedalling one-legged? Was I doing it just because it made me feel better, because I was used to doing seven hours a day and the Olympics were coming up and I desperately needed to feel like I was doing something? Or should I have a complete rest, so that at least I was fresh when I got back?

Maybe I should have taken myself away on holiday. As an athlete you have an in-built compulsiveness to train. Everything about you is crying out to exercise, and when you can't your body reacts in strange ways – you feel grumpy, achy, out of sorts.

But our physio was fantastic. She put together a programme of exercises that I could do and then came round to the house to do it with me, even on weekends – light gym work, some weights on the leg muscles we were trying to keep strong.

It was reported a few times that I'd considered retirement. That wasn't quite true. It was more that Jonny was joking that I nearly retired fifty times a day when I was in my more negative spells.

And it did get pretty bad. It wasn't so much 'I hate sport, I want to quit' as the frustration of wanting to do it more than anything else in the world but not being able to. I could have gone out on my bike or gone running, but my injury wouldn't have got any better, and I wouldn't have been able to perform. It was that frustration that was killing me – by trying to perform to the best of my ability, I got injured and could stay injured. All I wanted was to be outside and active.

There is a jealousy of everyone around you who isn't injured. You watch them going off on their bike and think: do you really appreciate how lucky you are not to have this? Jonny was getting ready to race. He was doing cross-country events and thinking about his first World Series outing. I struggled with that.

The only way I could deal with it was to cut myself off from it all. Don't watch cross-country races. Don't look at the results. Don't ask how the race was. Pretend it isn't happening, and the pain of being excluded from it won't be quite as bad. It might all be happening still, but it has no bearing on me.

I know now that Jonny took my lack of interest in his racing as jealousy of his achievements. He wasn't quite right; I was certainly jealous, but jealous only that I wasn't racing too.

It was almost as if the Olympics had nothing to do with me, and never would.

Coming Back Hard

ALISTAIR

The first thing Jonny said to me when I got injured was, 'Well, that's you done for this year, isn't it?'

He didn't mean it to sound as it did. There was humour there, although he's not a sympathetic person, and he's quick to blame you for your injuries. Yet I'm not even sure he was doing it on purpose; I think it was that pressure working on him, and I think, as the year turned out, some of it was actually very good for him.

In March, two weeks after the boot came off, the Achilles was still getting horribly swollen. At night it would be up like a balloon. I'd look down at it and think: oh hell – what have I done? This was just as I was trying to step up the amount of biking I could do. I was desperate to go out with the rest of the lads for long rides, but I could feel the injury on almost every pedal stroke.

I was so worried. I was thinking: what if I've done it again? I'll have to spend even more time in the boot. Time is running out. What about the Olympics? What if I can't make it?

I took the train down to London to do an appearance for one of my sponsors. Even on the way down it blew up. I went in to see the doctor who had done the original scan. He had a look and delivered his verdict: it's fine.

It was hard to believe him. It still looked so big and bad, and when it swelled up the pain really kicked in. My dad's explanation was that when I sat down and had my feet below hip height, fluid would pool in the injured area.

From that point on I kept it elevated whenever I could. Watching TV I'd have it up. Eating my tea I'd have it up. Sitting in the car I'd try to keep it up.

In early March we decided to get an underwater treadmill. It's an impressive piece of equipment: a temporary swimming pool that you build up in your back yard, the treadmill submerged within it, so you can run without the full effect of gravity and so return to exercise far earlier than you otherwise could. Its first positive effect came with just constructing the thing. I still had the protective boot on, but housemate Alec and I got to work digging away at the garden to clear enough space to put the base down.

Just that simple change of having something constructive to do with my time made me feel more positive – just digging a hole. It would now be possible to ride a little, and swim. About ten days after the boot came off I was able to hit the underwater treadmill. But there was still a hyper-sensitivity around the injured area. Any athlete who's been injured will recognize these symptoms: you are conscious of every little sensation, every tiny tweak and twitch. The paranoia is awful – have I done it again? Is it healing fast enough? Should it really be looking like that?

There were still scares. When I returned to doing hard running sessions my calf on that left side would get really sore. I'd have to stop and quit sessions, and that's an awful feeling. But the fact the doctor had given it the all-clear, and told me to expect it to be tender, to be sore and to look swollen, made me feel a lot better about it. When it got ugly again I kept the faith.

JONNY

I knew as we came into spring 2012 that at least I was in shape.

I'd had the best cross-country season of my life, and that was a great indication that the engine was tuned and firing. At the Inter-Counties – the toughest national-level race in the country – I came fifth, coming up against guys who were pure runners rather than triathletes. One of the scalps I took was the guy who had been the class act of the cross-country scene for years. As a kid competing in the Yorkshire Championships, loving being part of that scene and watching the seniors destroy the course, I had watched him beating everyone else by a full minute. To finish in front of him as a senior was one of those moments when you say to yourself: Jonny, you're doing okay here.

I flew over to San Diego, my first World Series event of the season, feeling optimistic. I knew I was fitter than I had ever been before, but you are never quite sure how that will translate into racing. Has everyone else had similarly strong winters? Was I just maturing as an athlete, but to a level below that of my rivals?

Training can only ever tell you part of the story. I hadn't raced a triathlon for seven months. Had I trained too much? Had I got the balance right – had my swimming and biking progressed in line with my running, or were those cross-country performances the result of too much focus on run sessions at the expense of the other two disciplines?

This year was different to any other. For the first time, with Alistair off the scene, I was unable to compare my performances to his. His Achilles injury meant that our training schedules were quite different. His results had always been my benchmarks, usually ones that I could only aspire to. Without him there I felt as if I knew very little – what shape I was in for triathlon, what tactics I might choose, how I should race.

There was one thing I knew: because the battle was still on between the other British athletes for the third spot in the Olympic team behind us two Brownlees, the racing would be frenetic and hard to control. Will Clarke, Tim Don, Stuart Hayes and others were still all fighting for that single place.

Would British Triathlon be convinced enough of their podium potential that they would select one on merit? Or would they decide that Alistair and I were the only two with a genuine chance of winning a medal? If it was the latter, they might decide instead that the third man should play a domestique role to support us, protecting us from breaks and working hard for us on the swim and bike. Then we'd be in the best possible shape for the scrap for gold.

ALISTAIR

I would have to drag myself out of bed – literally – to get to swimming sessions. And as I hobbled downstairs Jonny would be running out through the door, deliberately not waiting for me, so he could get to the pool first.

My reaction in the moment was anger. What a little git! 'Jonny, I've got a busted Achilles!' Everything I've done for him, and he's not even prepared to wait one minute to take me to swimming!

Then I would pause, take a step back and think: what more powerful motivation could there be than this, your own brother trying to get one over you when you've got a snapped Achilles? I knew then that Jonny constantly pushing me down, giving me no help at all was actually a positive stimulus.

Had I stopped and thought about it, I would have realized that there was nothing intentionally nasty about his behaviour. It was just Jonny being Jonny, always wanting to be on time. And he had a gold medal to try to win too.

It helped that my girlfriend, Flick, an Aussie triathlete, was around. She completely understood the demands on my time, and as an international athlete she had her own intense training workload too. She knew that she might not see me for days on end, or that I would sometimes be so tired that I wouldn't have the strength or desire to go out and do the normal things that other couples would do.

When I was going through dark times with the injury it was a huge help that she was there. When things are going well, as with anything in life, your relationship tends to be easy; but when you're struggling, the strength of it really shines through. I could get away from the full-on sport environment with her; I could escape the all-male atmosphere in the house and training group and get a more obvious level of support than you get from a load of blokes.

She also understood that resting, for a triathlete, means exactly that – sitting on your arse or lying down. It doesn't mean going out for a meal or strolling round the shops. She knew I wasn't letting her down if I didn't want to go out. She would do exactly the same – 'I'm knackered. I need an early night.' It might not be the most conventional relationship, but as an Olympic athlete your life is shaped in these strange ways.

JONNY

I arrived in San Diego without any real thought of whether I could come first, or second. And this time I was on my own in the hotel and in the hours leading up to the hooter.

Every single time I had raced in the previous season Alistair had been there. While ostensibly we may have been rivals, he was always an enormous help: he could calm me down, keep me smiling, be a friendly face to have around when the pressure and attention began to really build.

Going through all the familiar elements of a big race weekend without him felt alien. Sitting on my own during the pre-race briefing, going back to an empty hotel room by myself. I knew it was good for me, part of maturing as an athlete and a person, but I still found myself phoning him a few times – to talk tactics, what I should do at what point, how I should handle all the tension that was building around qualification for the Olympics.

San Diego is a difficult course – starting on the beach, a sea swim, a tough ride round Mission Bay and all in warm weather. You know what? None of that matters when you're locked into a race. The sightseeing can come later.

It began well for me. The swim was a straightforward one – no problems, feeling good – and on the bike we managed to get away in a little group. Coming into the run I knew my legs were in shape, and early on I started to go away from the rest, only for South Africa's Richard Murray to close in and get on to my heels.

At 4 kilometres I started to work harder and use all those cross-country training sessions to my advantage. A two-second lead stretched to four, and then eight, and then up to fifteen with Murray dropping back, but around 8 kilometres I found I had another problem – Sven Riederer, who had come past Murray at a canter and was now locked on to me.

Now the doubts kicked in. Had I gone off too hard? Am I fit enough? Has everyone else got faster while I have actually got slower? I felt genuinely scared. What did I have left? Sven and

Richard had both raced twice already that year. Would that help them or me?

Only at 9 kilometres, 1,000 metres from the finish line, did those fears start to subside. Maybe the adrenaline and fears had worked to my advantage, because I looked round to see I had re-established the lead and taken it out as far as twelve seconds again. That is a useful cushion to have at that stage in a race.

The main thought in my head was one of immense relief: thank God for that. Work hard to the line, make sure you get across it before you relax, and get there as quick as you can.

It took a while for it to sink in. This was my first major senior win, but with both Alistair and Javier Gomez missing. I also knew that it would all pale in comparison with the prize that lay in wait later in the year. Who would remember San Diego after the Olympics? This was a stepping stone – one that was brilliant to reach, but in itself no more than part of a much bigger and more important journey.

ALISTAIR

Achilles injuries are among the worst you can have for that level of unpredictability. One minute they can be fine; the next they're swollen and sore. Not having any influence over it is awful when you're an athlete obsessed with being in control. I've had stress fractures, and they're a breeze by comparison. You know how long they will take to heal, they heal, and you never feel them again.

Achilles injuries are never gone. They could come back at any point. And even as I started slowly returning to training, other problems began to surface.

My first decent session back was on the bike, a chain-gang

effort. I rode quite well. I could tell Jonny was saying to himself, 'Flipping prat, how has he done that? He's done no training, and yet he's still in that shape.'

Sure enough, he erupted. 'You're the biggest idiot in the whole group, you are!' And I thought: good, that's more motivation in the bank.

We did an interview for the BBC around May, three months before the start of the Olympics. Jonny told the interviewer how helpful he'd been when I was injured, how he'd waited to take me training, how he'd stopped to hold doors open for me. I was gobsmacked. My first reaction was disbelief – 'Clear off, Jonny!' But I think he actually believed it, or at least wanted to believe it.

JONNY

That injury, undeniably, caused problems for the two of us as siblings.

Most top-flight athletes tend to have a coach who is focused on supporting them alone. Their parents will also be completely focused on them, and their friends the same. Alistair and I don't have that. So when he was injured, he was in the unusual situation of having all his support group – coaches, friends, family – trying to get his main rival as fit and fast as possible. That's unique in triathlon, let alone Olympic sport.

Almost every athlete at the Olympics will have a team who want them to win more than they want anything else in the world. We don't, and Al thinks he has it even less than I do, because he's seen as the elder brother who is that much tougher and doesn't need any help. Whereas I'm the next one down, I'm younger, I'm not so confident. I don't want that to sound like either of us is complaining. Once you take away the emotional side of it, that's actually really good for us. It has made us self-sufficient. We don't look for praise and support.

The injury, however, was still our greatest test.

I don't know what he expected me to do. He's the sort of person who, had I gone up to him and asked him how he was, would tell me to piss off. He told me that I could have gone aqua-jogging with him. But I had my own races to do. I had my university dissertation to write. I couldn't go aqua-jogging because I didn't have any spare time.

While he was injured he had to put on a cast before he could go swimming. It took him ages, and he already left everything to the last minute. So as we got ready for our early morning swim he was always late. He wanted me to wait for him, which was making me late, day after day. I felt like he wasn't showing me enough respect.

I also had other races to focus on.

The emotional energy you expend at these big events is almost as big a factor as the physical exertion. When you get home, jet-lagged to hell as well, you're in bits. With the next World Series race after San Diego just two weeks later it felt as if I barely rested. But I knew the Madrid course suited me almost perfectly – a tough, hilly bike that would separate out the good riders from the bad and leave me – hopefully – in prime position coming into the run. The field for this was tougher too – it was the first time I'd be up against the Russian duo of Alexander Bryukhankov and Dmitry Polyanskiy, strong, silent types who never spoke to you and never smiled.

A little group of us got away a fraction on the swim – nine or so, led out by Richard Varga, nothing to rip up the race tactics, just enough for an encouraging feeling going through transition one. On the bike, all working incredibly hard, all hitting our turns at the front, opening up a lead of about forty seconds over the second group at the top of the big hill on the first lap and extending it on every lap we rode.

By the sixth lap we had it out to one minute thirty; a really hard effort on the final one took us into the run two minutes clear of the huge pack in pursuit. I looked around at the other guys and went through them one by one: Bryukhankov won't be able to out-run me after that; I can run faster than Aurélien Raphaël; I can run faster than Maik Petzold.

I went out hard. Bryukhankov held me to around five seconds for the first two or three kilometres, but after that I just went away.

The strangest thing about it was how easy it all felt. The bike had felt good, and the hardest part on the run was the first lap. From that point on I just felt better and better. Even as I ran round I was thinking: should it really feel this easy? This is all a bit weird.

You almost find yourself wondering if you've done something wrong – missed out a lap somewhere, or taken the wrong route. It was both pleasant and freaky.

There was another disconcerting element to it all. You train so hard that you always want to race to the best of your ability. You want to go as fast as you can for as long as you can. Well, winning Madrid felt so easy that I didn't have to. There was no stimulus to really push myself as hard as I could because I was winning comfortably while running comfortably. It almost felt like I had cheated myself. Why wasn't I working harder?

Alistair was hardly fulsome in his praise when I got back to Bramhope. There was, however, one huge advantage to him of my success in the first part of Olympic year: I was the perfect benchmark.

If you're coming back from injury and you can measure

yourself, every single day, against the current best triathlete in the world, it's a dream situation. Not only are you training with him, but you can see yourself gradually overtaking him. He could tell exactly where he might come by looking at his performance at home against me and then seeing how I was doing against our rivals in races. He knows exactly how fit his biggest rival is, he knows his psychology inside out.

Would he have wanted Gomez winning in San Diego and Madrid instead of me, or some other twenty-two-year-old he knew very little about? Had I been from Germany, I'm certain my success would have been much harder for him to take.

I think too I took a lot of pressure off him in the build-up to London. While he was injured, I could go to the World Series races and shape, for want of a better word, who we would be racing against and how. In Madrid an unplanned consequence of getting a little group away on the bike was that Tim Don and Will Clarke had no chance of making the top three, and so no chance of making the British team for the Olympics. That in turn meant it was much more likely that British Triathlon would give that third spot to an athlete who would act as a domestique for us – working flat out on swim and bike to get us in the perfect position to win it off the run. So Alistair could turn up for the Olympics knowing that he had the ideal team around him to help him win gold.

It went further. Because of the way we shaped the race in Madrid, other athletes who were perfect rivals for us, because they were strong swim–bikers but not as good as us on the run – Petzold, from Germany, and Varga from Slovakia – also qualified for their respective countries. Entirely inadvertently, it meant the Olympic environment could not have been better suited for Alistair, and he hadn't had to do anything about it.

ALISTAIR

The British Triathlon selection policy had been explained to us almost a year and a half before the final team selection was made. It was made quite clear to us what we had to do: get two podium finishes in World Series events in 2011 to guarantee selection. If you didn't you were at risk – it would be subjective, and up to the BTF who they picked and why. You would go either as a medal contender, or as someone who would aid the medal contenders – in other words, a domestique. There was a little bit of wriggle room – if a young guy came through very late but had the class, he might be given dispensation. But for the established athletes it was all in their hands.

We all understood what was needed, and as athletes we had fed into the process. Zara Hyde-Peters, head of the BTF, even came out to the World Series race in Sydney and talked us all through it. No one complained about it or expressed second thoughts.

As soon as the idea of picking a domestique as third man was raised I thought it was a good one. I felt Jonny and I would qualify – all we had to do was exactly what we had done in the previous few years – and I was confident we could do it. I liked the hard-nosed nature of it: it was completely about performance rather than taking part.

Let's send the team with the best chance of winning medals. Simple. By making it clear that you had to be one of the best in the world to make the team, it set the bar high. You had to strive for excellence or you would fall short. UK Athletics had talked about the same thing: only the top people should go to championships. If the BTF's policy made six guys fight harder than they had ever done before, that had to be a good thing. Once they're there, help them out as much as you can.

There was another aspect to it. Having Will or Tim in the same race could actually make it harder for us. We swim and bike well, so our rivals are always chasing us down from behind. If we had other Brits leading that charge they could tow through some very dangerous competitors.

On any given day, between Jonny and I we had an almost 100 per cent chance of winning a medal. That's a good shot for a team. If you have someone in the team who has only 10 per cent chance, but could accidentally pull through a Sven Riederer or Richard Murray – someone who could pip British athletes to a medal – it doesn't make logical sense. Even without factoring in all the advantages of a domestique that's already a sum worth thinking about.

Maybe the BTF should have been more proactive about selecting a domestique. They could have committed to it once we had qualified at the end of the 2011 season – in September. We had used pseudo-domestiques in the past; both Harry Wiltshire and Phil Graves had performed that sort of role for us.

Jonny, the coaches and I talked and talked about it. Had the BTF gone with it then, all the anger and recriminations that came later might have been avoided. It also would have meant more guys committing to it, giving a wider range of options to choose from.

The more Jonny and I talked about it too, the more we felt we knew who we wanted that domestique to be: Stuart Hayes.

JONNY

That ruthless side of sport was a strange thing to experience. As I rode at the front of the little breakaway group in Madrid,

I realized that my move to win the race unintentionally meant that Will and Tim had no chance of getting back into contention – and that, in turn, meant I was ending their dreams of racing in London. They had dedicated their lives to racing at the Olympics. Tim had barely seen his young daughter Matilda all year because he was trying to qualify. It was a horrible thought.

The decision from British Triathlon to pick a domestique was a brave one. In some ways it wasn't very British – in that it was all about an absolute dedication to success. But it was completely fair. The selection criteria had been set out months in advance, and everyone knew what they had to do to qualify. If they couldn't do that, they missed out. No one cheated them.

ALISTAIR

I did feel sorry for a lot of people, because I could see what was going to happen. But I was certain that everyone knew the rule about two podium finishes. I also knew that people would believe they would get those top-three finishes, because athletes tend by their nature to be optimistic. But when the others failed to deliver in a relatively weak race in Sydney it was clear that it wasn't going to happen at all.

Sometimes as a professional athlete you can be quite self-delusional. Once they failed to get a podium finish in Sydney, perhaps a few thought, okay, that hasn't happened but they'll probably relax the criteria a touch now, even though the selection policy was completely transparent.

The policy was tough. Guys had been training incredibly hard for four years and making huge sacrifices. But as an athlete, that's what you have to go through. The difference is how you view it all. I hope, had I been in their situation, that I would have taken responsibility and admitted that it was my fault.

I knew the criteria, I missed them and so I'm not going – or, I missed them, therefore I can go as a domestique and I will do everything in my power to be the best domestique possible. If you fail to meet a target that you have known about for eighteen months then it is no one else's fault. Harsh, but that's how I see it.

As it worked out, Stu soon seemed the perfect choice, and he meshed with us really well in June and July as we prepared for the Olympics.

The ideal domestique had to be an excellent swimmer and strong on the bike, but another big part of it was how much we could trust him, and how much he would commit to the role.

With someone like Stu it was impossible to know all that at the time. He's a great racer and has loads of experience; physically he ticked all the boxes. The question mark over him was how much we could trust him, and then how he might fit in with both our training plans and our domestic scene. Would he be okay about spending four weeks up a mountain with us in Switzerland?

What really disappointed me was that, when Stu's selection was announced, some people decided to blame the BTF or the selection criteria but not themselves. You heard things like, 'I did everything I could and I still wasn't selected,' when that just wasn't true.

People missed the bar. It wasn't that the bar was hidden. When you think how harsh the criteria were for some other sports, triathletes got off easily. UK Athletics didn't take three female 800 metre runners even though they all had the A standard asked for. Sport is all about setting goals and achieving them. If you achieve that goal you get selected. Some triathletes didn't achieve that goal; they didn't get selected. It can be that simple.

I can see why it became emotive – there's logic to thinking

the third best triathlete should get the third slot in the team. But there's no logic if that wasn't the selection policy.

There's a difference between getting to the Olympics just to be there, and getting to the Olympics to perform. That's something that not all the public understand. Selection should be a bump on the road, not a destination in itself.

I remember talking to Simon Whitfield, the first-ever Olympic triathlon gold medallist, before I raced in Beijing. He told me that he made sure he was good enough not to have to worry about qualification, which was another way of saying that if you're good enough to win a medal, you will be selected without having to think about it.

THE BROWNLEE WAY

BODY

JONNY You might imagine that we eat an incredibly disciplined, scientific diet. Well, some elite triathletes do, but we don't. Ordinarily we'll eat such normal food that some people are shocked – Coco Pops, meat pies, cakes – and that changes only a little when we're in competition. We'll always eat three big meals a day, wherever we are.

When we travelled the length of the country for races as kids, Dad would always take us to a pizza restaurant the night before competition. That was the accepted routine. Dad told us it worked because there were lots of carbohydrates in the pizza base and plenty of salt, and very little that can go wrong.

Some of our rivals will eat only rice before races, because they tried it once and raced well off it. But this can't always work, and if you race in many different places you might not always be able to get the ingredients you depend on. So Al and I have never developed habits like these. And that's a good thing, because it means our preparations won't be ruined because we're unable to lay our hands on the exact food we want.

When I was sixteen and raced in my first French Grand Prix there was an obsession in my team with something they called 'energy cake'. They were all banging on about it – you have to eat this before a race, you simply must. They insisted the hotel chef cooked up a special batch. After they'd set off for the race they realized they'd left the cake at the hotel. This cake was so important to them that they had to send a mechanic back to get it. Madness.

ALISTAIR What probably surprises amateur triathletes, runners and cyclists about our training schedule is how little recovery we appear to have. We do so many sessions a week that it seems as if there is no rest at all, and an awful lot of volume there.

Traditionally there is a trade-off between the intensity of your training and the odds of you getting injured. Put simply, the harder and more intense your training, the greater the strain you are putting on your body. Well, our unusually skewed ratio is a conscious decision. I could train a bit less, and I'd get less injured, but I wouldn't be as good. Or I could train as much as I do, take the risk of being injured and be the best I can.

I have questioned that approach a lot when I've been injured and unable to train. I enjoy doing it all so much that I had to ask myself if it was worth sacrificing being able to do any of it for long periods so I can compete with the very best. Do I want to succeed so much that I'm prepared to miss doing what I love doing every day?

Here's the thing: I'd rather be as good as I can be, and maybe have a shorter career through injury, than never know, or cruise. It's always been about how good I can be. How hard can I push it? How much training can I do, how fast does that make me? I'd prefer to have three or four cracking years of winning stuff than have ten years of being average, and I know Jonny's exactly the same.

JONNY A lot of what makes you good also makes you injury-prone. Al is a little leaner than me, carries a bit less muscle. He has also always been about running, cycling and swimming. I played football and cricket as well, and as a rugby player I was a fly-half. All three of those involve moving in multiple directions and getting beaten up. I broke pretty much all my fingers when I was young. That more varied sporting background has given me better all-round strength.

There seems to be a weird symbiosis between the two of us with injuries. When I got a stress response in my femur, it was about two weeks after Al got a stress fracture. I went to have a scan entirely because Al had his injury. If I hadn't, my injury wouldn't have been picked up, and I would have developed a stress fracture too.

ALISTAIR I think I have the sort of body type that can keep going and going, until something breaks. I'm stringier and leaner than Jonny, and so probably a little more flexible, while Jonny is more powerful. Things tighten up with him, which is a restriction on how efficiently he can work. I have fewer restrictions so I can keep going and going – but then something serious happens, like the stress fracture I had at the start of 2010.

Despite those injuries, all these brutal sessions – all these hours in the pool, or out on the bikes in winter, or throwing up your guts after running sessions – build an air of invincibility around us. Why? Because the most important feeling you can have going into a big race is the knowledge that you have done everything you possibly can to be in the best possible shape. And it doesn't matter if you've been injured. It's never nice being on the start line and thinking: what if I hadn't had that injury? But you take it as a given that you've been injured, and change those negative thoughts into: I've done everything I can, considering I was injured. You don't think about your rivals too much, and whether they're injured. That has no effect on me whatsoever – I just don't care. The important thing is that I'm here, and that I'm ready to race.

MIND

JONNY I'm often asked if we get bored of so much training. Well, you do hit thresholds sometimes, and some sessions are more enjoyable than others. When you do a hard ride on a Saturday morning, get back home and crash out watching *Football Focus*, it's very hard to make that first step back out of the door. On certain days you think: it would be absolutely great to be able to watch Leeds United today, rather than train. You find yourself wishing for a different life. But you know as soon as you made that change you'd be desperate to get training again. I'm so stuck in our training routine that if I didn't get up early on a Thursday morning and go swimming, for example, my brain wouldn't know what was going on.

You find ways round the boredom. On Friday Leeds Rhinos rugby league team often play. So my motivation is to get my training done early and then go to Headingley to watch the game. It gets me away from triathlon, and takes my mind away from it all.

ALISTAIR I love training more than anyone, but you can't just train. You have to remember that you do it to race. You see countless examples of people who just train for its own sake. They go out, do the miles, come back tired and feel good about themselves, not because they've won some race. To me that's completely back to front.

You're never sure with triathlon whether it attracts obsessive people in the first place or it makes you obsessive, but the relationship is there regardless. It's the same with lots of endurance sports. I see it with some women – they can sometimes get more addicted to exercise than men – and with the bright ones in particular. At school a teacher used to say to us, 'Ah, it's always the smartest lads, the ones doing best at school, who run. They work the hardest.'

You need that obsession to a certain degree. I never wake up wishing I could lead an entirely different life. Never. Sometimes when I get bored I can certainly lose my sense of enjoyment – you realize you're doing it for the sake of routine rather than fun. But that will be the moment when another sense kicks in, one which says, 'I have to do this to be the best.'

It's not a job for me, and it's not a hobby. It's my passion. It's what I love doing.

When I'm injured, I'm not sitting there thinking that I want to get fit, particularly, or that I want to race or train; I'm just thinking that I want to get out on my bike. I'm so frustrated having to sit there when I could be out running or cycling.

Doing sport to perform at the elite level can take away the fun of just doing it. Occasionally, when it's really hurting, you wonder if you'd be better off doing a skill-based sport, like being a spin bowler. But I'm shocking at cricket.

JONNY I've trained next to divers before. I know they do train hard, but fundamentally they just dive into water, don't they? I'll watch them when I'm slogging up and down the swimming pool and feel a touch aggrieved. But what's great about the sport we do is a simple equation: what you put in, you get out. In a skill-based sport it's nowhere near as straightforward. When I played football there were some lazy lads who still had the best touch you'd ever seen. If you're lazy in triathlon you won't even get started.

ALISTAIR People ask me about pressure. Pressure? The actual race is the fun part. You train so flipping hard that the race is the best bit – you look forward more than anything to having a few easy days and getting to a race, because it's not your normal training.

That is as true for something as incomparable as the Olympics as it is for a tiny local race. We probably put as much pressure on ourselves to win at something like the Bunny Run, that fell race near Haworth every Easter, or to beat someone's school record at Bradford Grammar School, as we do at a World Championships.

We were always that intense from a young age. We never thought, it's a Yorkshire under-thirteens, it doesn't really matter. I always put a lot of pressure on myself in every race and I could always take it. I remember standing on the start line at a World Junior Championships, everyone around me saying, 'Oh my God, this is serious . . .' and yet to me it was just another race. It wasn't that I ever dumbed down races; it's that I've consistently put massive pressure on myself to win them.

FROM A TO BROWNLEE

Be Consistent

JONNY It can be hard getting the regular training hours in when you're holding down a job. But there's no point in doing a huge amount of training one week and very little the next. You're better off doing four weeks of fifteen hours each rather than doing alternate weeks of thirty hours and five hours. That's true of both the volume of your training and its intensity.

Train With Others

ALISTAIR Even at our level it's so much easier training hard and well when you're doing it with someone else. If I know I can meet a friend at the track to do a hard session together it makes it seem possible, when otherwise I would just be thinking about how hard it was going to be. This is even more important when you're working. If you're getting in from work at five thirty p.m., knackered and hungry, you're much more likely to go running if you've got a date with your mate to do it together. And once you have a routine together, it's fixed in the diary.

Set Goals

JONNY We're lucky in that we've always enjoyed what we do. But it's a huge help to have a target in your mind. When you're working really hard in training, hurting yourself, you need to know why you're doing it – because you're racing in two weeks' time, and you want to be in the best possible shape. Set lots of short-term goals too. In April 2012 I wasn't thinking about the Olympics; I was thinking about a Grand Prix event taking place in France in May.

Mix It Up

ALISTAIR Make sure you build variety into your training plan. That might mean mountain-biking, that might mean a training camp. People sometimes imagine that training has to be mentally hard to be physically hard. It doesn't. A boring 50-mile ride is not more effective than a fun one. It doesn't matter if, because you're running with a group, you end up going a little slower. Mix it up. Your body and your mind need it. We add diversity by training in different places – 50 weeks of identical training from October sounds horrendous. Some people seem to think variety is for the weak-minded; I think the opposite is almost true. Repetition is for the weak-minded.

Prepare For Anything

ALISTAIR You want to be able to deal with whatever fate throws at you during a competition. Jonny will always take a spare pair of goggles and two wetsuits. One might rip; one might feel better on than the other. Take spare laces. I normally pack two pairs of racing trainers. Although sometimes that has caused problems – I have run up and down transition before the race, one shoe from each pair on my feet, trying to decide which ones to choose.

Race as You Train

JONNY Try to avoid doing anything new on your big day. Use the equipment you're used to, eat the food you're used to. I remember when I was younger deciding to use a new carbon seat-post for a race. I think Alistair had been given it – the expense and technology behind it blew my mind. I jumped on my bike after transition one and the thing snapped. And this was during a qualifying race for the Great Britain team. I tried cycling with my backside resting on it gently, but the whole saddle fell off. Race over.

Listen to Your Body

ALISTAIR A training plan should never be set in stone. It can only be a guide, to be shaped by how you are feeling on a particular day, the time you have and the goals you have set out. Holding back on training if you have a niggle or are feeling exhausted is not bottling it; it's being clever. Be confident in your own instinct, knowing that you're not going to damage your training and your eventual performance. Take heed of other seasoned riders and runners around you and realize you don't have to ride five hours every Sunday. If it's raining you might ride for two hours, and then do a bit more another day. Listen to your body. Listen to your brain.

Do Something Rather Than Nothing

JONNY Some amateur triathletes are short of time, and they struggle to see the point of going out for a half-hour run if their training schedule tells them they need to do an hour and a half. There is a point. Get the training in however you can. Do a half-hour run twice a week if you can't find time or motivation for a one-hour run.

Make It Fun

ALISTAIR In one sense training should always be serious. We are putting ourselves through intense physical discomfort in order to win a competition as important as the Olympics. At the same time, unless you are actually enjoying the day-to-day slog, you will struggle for motivation. The prize at the end of the long road will always be there, but when you're out in the freezing cold rain in January it's impossible to keep going by imagining racing on a warm summer's day in Hyde Park.

That doesn't mean that you don't work your arse off in the session; it's about your attitude within it. You can be riding along and decide, hold on, this is too slow, we shouldn't be riding at this pace, and then think instead, actually, don't worry about it, if we want to be riding at this pace to the next signpost or down the hill, what's the harm? The pressure to add that little extra – the obsession with doing another ten minutes – well, what's the advantage if that's going to have a psychological disadvantage? Just enjoy the ride or the run for what it is.

Run to discover your local area, to see what's down that street or in those woods. Run to college or work, arriving awake and invigorated, training rather than commuting. Mix up your favourite routes; if you're limited by your environment, reverse your usual one. You'll be amazed how fresh it can feel. Enjoy the sensation of moving at pace using only your body, of listening to the sounds of your surroundings, of breathing easily and gliding along in a rhythm all of your own.

The Final Countdown

ALISTAIR

In early June I tested my fitness at a low-key race at Blenheim with Jonny and felt okay. It was time to step back on to the big stage and see what I had.

The next World Series race was in Kitzbühel on 24 June, six weeks before the men's race in London. I knew I was in pretty good shape – I'd managed to get a good solid block of training behind me, and that's where my confidence always comes from. But you're never quite sure how that will translate in racing conditions.

JONNY

The old doubts still lingered beneath the surface despite the big wins in San Diego and Madrid. Did it all really count when the two leading triathletes of the past four years, Alistair and Gomez, weren't there? Was this actually all a mirage? Was my fitness not actually all that good? Come the Olympics would those wins not matter? Everyone was telling me what great form I was in; I was almost the only one who didn't believe it.

Kitzbühel would answer all those questions. For the first time all the big boys were racing. Alistair was back; Gomez was racing his first World Series event.

You'd think that would put more pressure on me, but instead

I felt relieved. What did I have to lose? I was more relaxed than I had been in either of the two previous races.

I knew Alistair was in good shape. Watching him train every day I could see that his running was coming back well. He'd started putting together some rapid sessions and was looking like the Al of old. I didn't quite believe he was going to beat me, but I thought it would be close, far closer than it had been the season before.

I was genuinely excited to be in that situation. I was even more pumped when Al and I came out of the swim and immediately put a break away on the bike with another one of the Russians, Ivan Vasiliev. Al must have been full of adrenaline in his comeback race, because even with Vasiliev just hanging on for the tow rather than doing any work we had a lead of 25 seconds early on. God, it hurt. And the more it hurt, the smaller the gap became. Behind us the German Olympic trio of Jan Frodeno, Steffen Justus and Maik Petzold were driving on the pursuit and closing us down to nothing.

I looked at Al and gasped, 'What the hell are we doing here? We're smashing ourselves to bits, and for what? You can run fast, I can run fast. We don't need to do this.' Sure enough, the pack caught us. I was shattered, and furious. 'Alistair, what have you done here? You've screwed this up now. We're stuffed, and everyone else with their fresh legs will hammer us on the run.'

ALISTAIR

To me it felt pretty close to the ideal situation. We were away on the bike with a guy we both knew we could beat on the run. What's not to like about that? But when the main pack hauled us back in, the tactics had to change – and that was when Stu Hayes came into his own.

There's a big risk at that point, when you've been away and working hard, that as soon as you're reeled back in people will start to attack you – hard. It's cruel but makes perfect sense. Why wait for your rival to recover? Strike when he is at his weakest, when his legs are shot.

What Stu could do was go to the front of the group and keep the pace high enough to discourage breaks, but not so fast that we couldn't hang on. Instead we could sit on his wheel or close in, recuperate, keep an eye on everyone else, ready to go hard again when it came to the run.

I had no idea how I would feel on the run. I made a conscious decision not to go out too hard because it was warm and I had sufficient doubts about my fitness to know it could easily get a bit nasty. So my first 2 kilometres were a controlled effort.

JONNY

Alistair had a fantastic second transition and was out on the run with a two-second lead over me. Straight away I ran past people too and found myself in second place. I expected to feel rough but there was a freshness and bounce in my legs that I'd never dreamed could be there.

Alistair was out in front, and Gomez was soon on my shoulder. The last thing I wanted to do was drag Gomez up to my brother, so I stuck in a little acceleration and got rid of him by about 2 kilometres. The chase was on. A lap in I had closed to within four seconds of Alistair, but he began to stretch it and stretch it – back up to ten seconds, then fifteen, then twenty by the start of the fourth and final lap.

ALISTAIR

I expected Jonny to run back up to me, maybe even with Gomez in tow. When I extended that time gap again I gradually began to feel really good. I couldn't quite believe it was happening. I was thinking, wow – it can't get much better than this!

In other races I probably would have eased off a little at that point. Once your lead is twenty seconds that close to the line, you know you are likely to stay clear. But this time I kept pushing it, in part because I was feeling good, but even more because at last I could.

JONNY

That's when I decided to stop working. Gomez was long gone. Alistair was too far ahead. I thought about the Olympics to come, just six weeks on, and the training camp in St Moritz, and I knew where my priorities should lie. We had been going into every race with no thought of the trials to come – just smash it, smash it as hard as you can – but now the sensible part of my brain kicked in.

For a split second I did wonder if I should give chase just to show him and the watching world that I was no longer the second Brownlee, that I was the brother who had won two big World Series races that year, but I knew I had to hold something back. Those two wins had already shown everyone what I could do; I would have other opportunities that summer to show them again.

Watching Al go away and win it in such style hit me hard. My first thought was an angry one. You stupid twat, I've trained my guts out all winter, you've been injured and have had two months off running, sat on your arse feeling sorry for yourself, sulking, talking about quitting and how much you hate sport – and now you've come out in your first race and destroyed us all, made us look like idiots. Screw you, I'm never going to feel sorry for you ever again.

I'd been nervous for him too, worried how he might cope if it all went wrong or if he was beaten in a way he'd never been beaten before.

As it began to sink in, the normality of the situation – Al dominant out in front, me chasing – made me feel a little better. Once logic kicked in I could see how his return to form would actually aid me – I'd have him as a benchmark again, to chase down, to bring me into similar form. There is no more effective tool than competing three times a day, every single day, with a guy who has just beaten you.

That win changed my brother's mood. Instantly he was more relaxed, much warmer towards me. When I could train and he couldn't it really hurt him. When he was back to beating me everything felt right in his world again.

ALISTAIR

Even at my most optimistic I wouldn't have seen it working out quite as well as it did. From the moment you dive in for a top-level swim you can never be quite sure how it might go. I've never finished outside the top six or seven in a triathlon swim, but the fear still crept in. Being able to push hard on the bike felt good, but it was always going to be the run that was the worry. When it went as well as it did, even with that hard biking in the legs, it was a rather wonderful surprise.

There were still moments when self-doubt would creep in.

I would find myself thinking of all the things that could go wrong. But to get Kitzbühel out of the way, in such dominant fashion, gave me a peace I hadn't experienced for months. I knew I was there. Had I produced that Kitzbühel performance at the Olympics instead, having got another big block of training under my belt, I'd have been content, so to perform that well that early was a wonderful surprise. Every athlete looks for a little boost as they come into the Olympics, and Kitzbühel gave me that boost.

Other athletes have a theory that you can be in too good shape too early, but I've never bought that. Try experiencing it the other way and then tell me that you'd rather be in bad form than good form. It's completely illogical. With the Olympics closing in fast, Kitzbühel was the perfect marker for me.

JONNY

With six weeks to go until race day in London, we left Austria and headed off to St Moritz.

As a training base that part of Switzerland had everything. There was a 25 metre pool a couple of kilometres round the valley in Pontresina. It was very Swiss. Spotlessly clean, very strict on what time you were allowed in and had to be out, and with spa pools and treatment rooms around the main pool. The running track was in the middle of the town, which was surrounded by mountains, and the cycling was amazing. If we needed to stay on the flat we could stick to the valley floor for 40 kilometres or so, and if we wanted to ramp it up then there were great climbs up the mountainsides.

We had used it twice before, and the strong Leeds vibe there – our support team and training partners were with us, and almost all of us hailed from West Yorkshire – made it a much more chilled place to be than the high-performance aspect of the camp might make you think.

What we also had this time was a near-perfect atmosphere. It was focused, but it was relaxed. Had you walked in you would never have guessed that it was a holding-camp before the biggest competition of our lives.

I almost expected something different. These were my first Olympics. Subconsciously I imagined everything would somehow be supercharged, but there was nothing new except a sense of relief: I haven't crashed, I'm not injured, I'm not ill.

Even the journey from Kitzbühel to St Moritz was relaxed. Alistair, in a clapped-out rental car, raced British Triathlon coach Ben Bright up the mountain. Our Leeds tri training partners were in the convoy; Richard Varga was there, the best swimmer in triathlon; our regular running mates were on board to give us someone to chase during track reps.

Then there was Stuart Hayes, already an intrinsic and essential part of the team. Even now, more than a month before the Olympics, he was with us totally – at our sides in every training session, eating with us, relaxing with us, using his experience to keep us calm. He would constantly warn us against over-training, being so cautious on our behalf that we nicknamed him Safety Stu. He may be the first person in history to insist on drinking bottled water in Switzerland.

The support team was perfect. Malcolm set the run sessions, keeping everything normal, holding us back when excitement or inexperience made us want to do too much. Jack was typically level-headed and even-handed.

It was a classic display of how the two of them work so well for us as coaches. Both Jack and Malcolm worked out a long time ago that the best way to succeed as an athlete is to make your own decisions. That's important. You have to stand on the start line at a race knowing that it's you who is responsible for what you're about to do. If you can stand there knowing you've done all you can do, that's very liberating.

Quite cleverly Malcolm and Jack took that step back so we would make ourselves responsible for our actions, yet they still make themselves available for little tips and pokes and prods. It can go wrong. If it does, you work out what you need to do to change it. By being in charge of the decisions ourselves we take ownership of them. We will always take lots of advice from the two of them, but the final say lies with us.

An example: Malcolm is very good at spotting issues before they crop up. He'll notice that we're looking a bit tired on a Tuesday night and suggest we ease off a little for the next few days. Similarly, if a race goes well on the Saturday we can turn up for a track session on a Tuesday night feeling bang up for it. Malcolm can spot that it's the adrenaline talking, and he'll know that what would actually be best for us is a rest.

I don't want to underplay what either Jack or Malcolm does today. Jack is responsible for all the swim sessions we do – whether he's physically there or not, he'll have written the training plan for that particular set. That set will then apply to the whole squad. Malcolm comes up with 100 per cent of the running sessions that we do on Tuesdays and Saturdays. He'll also introduce elements we wouldn't have thought of ourselves – drills, gym sessions. Outside those sessions Malcolm will help us to talk about what we do, but he won't tell us what to do.

Their support away from sport is brilliant. When I'm injured Malcolm attends appointments with me and discusses possible treatments. I can be completely confident that everything he advises me is in both my short-term and my long-term interests, rather than being about my own ego or the BTF's short-term interest.

Jack and Malcolm are low-maintenance coaches. They don't need their egos massaging. Some bigwig from British Triathlon once went up to Malcolm and said, 'Oh, very well done for making Alistair run so fast.' He replied, 'Don't be so ridiculous. I just stand there and watch.' You don't get many coaches like that.

Years ago, when we were kids on those northern triathlon camps, Jack could easily have insisted that we were coached by him. If he had, it would probably have ended there. He and Malcolm both realized how independent we are. I discovered the boundaries myself, and it has made me the athlete I am today. By trying to do everything and gradually realizing I couldn't, it made me want to seek out their advice. Then it was up to me to take the decision whether to act on that advice or not, rather than being told.

In St Moritz, Jack and Malcolm led a wider team. Physio Emma kept our bodies loose. Kelly the cook made sure there would be no repeat of our first trip to St Moritz, when the cost of food was such a cruel surprise that within three days Al and I had to phone Mum and Dad to ask them to ship out boxes of Fray Bentos pies to keep us going.

Ben Bright's attitude summed up the commitment we had from the team, something we were incredibly fortunate to have. Out on one of our long rides, he received a long-awaited phone call from back home telling him his heavily pregnant wife had gone into labour. He finished the ride, raced down the mountain to the airport, flew home and made the birth by fifteen minutes. Two days later he was back with us, a model of calm and support despite all that had happened.

For four weeks we did nothing but train bloody hard, eat and sleep. In the gaps we watched the Tour de France and Wimbledon on TV and played FIFA on my Xbox. With talk of the

Olympics building every day back home, we kept hearing from our parents of how the country was becoming obsessed – news stories about us on the main TV news, big documentaries on the radio, adverts we'd shot earlier in the year appearing on television and in magazines. To be insulated from it all was a huge help. It all felt so far away, even in the last fortnight before the opening ceremony. You wouldn't have known the Olympics were about to start. St Moritz was quiet, restrained and exactly as it had been on our two previous training camps there.

ALISTAIR

We knew our way round and we knew all the training routes. The first time we had trained in St Moritz the two of us were on our own, but the team had gradually developed until we had a really strong, well-balanced group around us. Having a cook and cleaner there made life even simpler, which was exactly the intention. It made you feel as if you weren't training and working that hard, even though we were, and doing it all at altitude.

Having gone through the whole Olympic experience in Beijing I knew how over-complicated it could so easily get. I felt that we had done a really good job in not having to deal with new routes, new people and unnecessary hassles.

We hadn't given too much thought to how it would feel being in Britain as the Olympic build-up really swung into gear. But once we were away in Switzerland I was incredibly grateful that we'd managed to dodge so much of it.

Being an Olympian has its place in your preparations. You need to feel keyed up and part of something much bigger than you. But to have that for the full six weeks before your race would be overwhelming. Having a constant reminder of what you will be going through can affect your thinking. You find yourself adding an extra ten minutes on to a run, or three more reps on the bike, when the best thing for you is to stick to your schedule and make sure you're as fresh on race day as you can possibly be. That's the balance you have to strike. You always want to squeeze in a little more to make yourself better than you were before, but if you overdo it you'll come crashing down the other side.

There were times when I would be lying in bed at night, the Olympics going round and round in my head. Then I would go from obsessing about the Olympics to obsessing about why I was obsessing about the Olympics. That's when the normality of your training regime comes to your rescue. Wake up, swim, go out on your bike, run. Nothing has changed. Look around you – there's Jonny, there's Alec, there's our mate Rhys. Nothing has changed.

What wasn't part of our planning was the way we dodged the worst summer West Yorkshire had seen in our lifetimes. The endless rain that caused all those floods in the countryside around us would have made our long rides and runs horrific, and some of them simply impossible. In St Moritz we barely had a day's rain. We could do exactly what we wanted to, when we wanted to.

At that point we began to wonder what would happen if the grey skies and torrential rain carried on through to the Olympics. While it would be miserable for the spectators, I thought it would be fantastic for us. Who could be more used to competing hard in horribly wet and cold weather than two lads born and raised in the north of England?

We knew that bad weather would put doubt in the minds of some of our rivals, and for others – even if it was just subconscious – they would be making excuses to themselves: I can't be expected to race well in these conditions; I don't fancy this; this is a nightmare for me, on the biggest day of my professional career. Even if it's drizzling there are ten guys I could name straight away who you could write off because of that.

There was one nagging problem: without noticing it, I had developed quite a sore hip and groin. It worried me a little, and then it worried me a lot. For a week I couldn't run without being in significant pain. I was sent for a scan, which brought good news and bad: the injury would be easily treated, and would soon pass; but I had an extra bone in my back. Don't ask me what it did apart from trigger the injury, but it's still there.

JONNY

The escape had worked perfectly for us. But we knew it had to end, and I was also secretly glad to get home. Being back in Leeds signalled that the Olympics were almost with us.

We had two weeks and one day to wait at home. We had some friends round to watch the opening ceremony, ordered in our usual – fish and chips – and tried to enjoy the spectacle rather than obsessing over our own role in what was to follow, but it felt weird. It was a dead time, a time for waiting, and wondering.

I just wanted the Olympics to arrive for us. Out on our usual chain gang, all I could think about was crashing. What happens if I fall off now, in this of all weeks, in all years? It rained and it rained, and with every drop my trepidation grew. Safety Stu warned us to be cautious, but I was already a man on the edge. On the Saturday before our race we rode out on our regular loop past Bolton Abbey and sat down in the café there. It was all so normal, yet so frighteningly different.

The Tuesday after we got back we had a tough track session – 5 x 1 kilometre – which went really well. I ran faster than ever.

I walked away from there thinking, we're pretty fit here. This feels good.

ALISTAIR

The Olympics were having an effect on us even 250 miles north, and not always in the way we expected. Our local track, the one we had trained at for years, was suddenly shut off by security guards. The Chinese team had taken it over.

There was one final near-disaster. Because of a football tournament being held at the usual venue for our Saturday running session, we were being hit in the face by footballs and harassed by tiny kids in luminous bibs. The surface is almost universally excellent, with the exception of one small but significant hole that's well hidden by grass. Jonny managed to fall into it twice. It wasn't quite how you might picture the final preparations of two elite athletes.

We had intended to leave the Olympics alone until we travelled down to London. We failed at that miserably. On the very first Saturday we changed the timing of our training so we could get home in time to watch the men's cycling road race; we then watched the women's road race on the Sunday, and from then on we abandoned any pretence of not caring about it.

While our race still seemed somehow separate from everything we were watching, we were becoming anxious – about a freak injury, about a sudden cold that might strike. All through that first week, even as we trained normally, the anxiety built and built.

Our race was on Tuesday 7 August. By the preceding Saturday, watching Helen Jenkins racing in the women's Olympic triathlon, the nerves were truly jangling.

We had spent a lot of energy worrying, even if subconsciously, about what might go wrong. Watching Helen have a bad swim – and Helen never misses a swim pack – added to that creeping unease. It took British Triathlon's head coach, Ben Bright, sitting down with us to explain that Helen had been carrying an injury to bring some calm and logic back to the situation.

JONNY

Never before have I been thinking about a race four days before it begins. Normally for a World Series race you haven't even flown to the host city by then.

Not many athletes travel to an Olympics by train, either, but that's exactly what we did on the Saturday night. That in itself felt strange, because it's a journey we have done so many times, and there are few places as mundane as a train station.

When we rolled into King's Cross we thought: right, London, Olympic host city, here we go. That was another surprise. It looked exactly as King's Cross always does. There was absolutely no indication that an Olympics was raging all around.

Even at our hotel, tucked away north of Hyde Park near Lancaster Gate, the mood was strange. We were greeted by familiar faces – coach Malcolm, physio Emma, our usual mechanic, Glen – but everyone was tired and a little flat after the women's race earlier in the day. We had stayed at the same hotel for the Hyde Park race the summer before, so even that felt completely lacking in Olympic glamour.

ALISTAIR

That had been a key decision – staying out of the Olympic village – and it worked a treat. The rooms were good, the food was good, the start of the race was a five-minute walk way. Also, by that very familiarity, it helped defuse those latent nerves.

The village was an hour's bus ride away. It was so huge that it took ten minutes to walk to the food hall, and it would take twenty minutes to get back out through security if you wanted to go training. There was extra stress everywhere you looked. To go swimming you had to go through security twice, so instead we stayed at the hotel, cycled across Hyde Park on our bikes and used the Imperial College pool in South Kensington. Perfect.

On Sunday 5 August, two days before the race, they held the race briefing. There we became aware for the first time of the tension our rivals were experiencing; at one stage we were asked to take out our race kit, so the officials could check for non-Olympic branding, and the gasps and looks when we brought out the specially designed, strange-looking white race helmets were reactions that spoke of paranoia – 'Oh no, they've got special helmets – they'll be even faster!'

JONNY

The pontoon draw was made. For me, that ratcheted up the nerves a little more. Gomez came first, being ranked top in the Olympic standings, but as the next athletes in line you have no idea which spot he's picked. The first clue you get is when the spot you subsequently ask for turns out to have been taken already. It's like playing Battleships. I hated it.

Alistair was fifth to choose, I was seventh. I wanted to start on one of the extreme sides so I could stay out of that horrible swimming melee. I asked for Slot One. 'Taken.' Then Slot Two. 'Taken.' Nerve-wracking.

Underlining that issue was the memory of how bad the swim leg had been in the Serpentine the previous summer. It had been brutal. We had watched the women's race and seen the chaos; Helen had told us that the first buoy had been like a car crash, and we didn't want the same thing to happen to us. So this was our thinking: the extreme right of the pontoon might not offer the shortest and thus fastest line to the first buoy, but it would be the safest.

As I looked around the room, I made mental notes on our rivals.

Gomez, without any weakness, possibly the first triathlete to be superb across all three disciplines, the greatest threat of all. Before we came along he was the fastest swimmer, the fastest cyclist, a runner who could change the pace and tear a field to shreds. I knew what he could do, and I knew how he would do it – running so close to your heels that he would actually clip your feet, showing the effort he was putting in by pushing his lips into a funnel shape and sucking hard. If he were to get in a breakaway on the bike without us, we would be in deep trouble. Doomsday scenario.

Sven Riederer, a tough man, maybe not so quick at the start of the race but capable of running an even-paced 10 kilometres when most others would be tying up and dying. I wanted to see him racing with his head tilted ever so slightly to one side. When he did that, we knew he was tired, and when he was tired, he would be beaten. But tactically he was excellent. He had worked out how, in theory at least, he could beat us – by holding his pace over the run while we might start fast and then fractionally drop away.

David Hauss, the Frenchman we heard had peaked perfectly for London. He could miss the lead pack on the swim and come nowhere, or hang on long enough to use his speed on the run to spring a surprise. If he was on our shoulders going into the final 1,000 metres, he would be a serious danger.

Richard Murray, young South African, an old rival from our junior duathlon days. Richard can run. But when he runs tired, you know. He comes up so close to you, so desperate not to let you go, that he will be clattering into your elbows.

There were more – the Russians, poker-faced, led by Alexander Bryukhankov – a hard man, the Terminator of triathlon, capable of continuing through hellish conditions. Old hands like Simon Whitfield, Olympic Champion twelve years before. There were threats around the room. We moved on.

The Monday passed quickly. A spin on the bikes round Regent's Park, a run round Hyde Park. The latter was an error. There we were, in full GB kit, all too recognizable. People were running after us, diving in front of us with phone cameras.

It felt intense, almost too much so. But it was nothing compared with what would follow the next morning.

Two Hours

ALISTAIR

And so it comes back to the beginning: the two brothers, standing side by side, the world and everyone we ever cared about looking on.

Eleven thirty a.m., 7 August 2012. A thin blue pontoon sticks out into the Serpentine. The hooter squeals, and into the dark waters we go.

As we surfaced and started to stroke hard, we began to put our carefully thought-out plans into place.

We had to keep it very simple, because it's all too easy to over-complicate your tactics in such a big race. Our training partner and friend, Slovakia's Richard Varga, wanted to split up the main pack on the swim; we wanted exactly the same. He wanted to be leading the race out of the water, but equally he knew that if he went flat out and came out of the water in an exclusive group of one then he'd go nowhere on the bike, because he would have to do all the work himself while others raced as a team. If he swam fast enough to pull a group of us away then we could take him somewhere on the bike.

As a result, the deal was clear: he'd swim as hard as he could to the first buoy, wait for someone to get on his feet, without worrying exactly who it was, and then keep swimming. We promised that we'd make sure we were there.

And we were, after a start that was even more frenetic than ever. Richard got his speed so spot on that he was even doing backstroke around that first buoy, having a cheeky look behind to make sure there was someone on his feet.

Before you start wondering what sort of shady deal this was, it was nothing more than logic. Those tactics were the perfect ones for Richard – he was acting entirely in his own interests. It just so happened that his racing interests tied in beautifully with ours.

Nor did it make the swim an easy one. After that first buoy we both had to hit it hard for a couple of hundred metres, because we were down in 15th and 16th. We needed to get past that big block of rivals and get up into the top five for the rest of our plan to come into play. What came to our rescue was that some of those guys in front of us had made the classic triathlon swimming error of going out too hard over the first 300 metres, of going deep into the red. Once that happens there's only one way to go – backwards. This was the Olympics; everyone was obsessed with getting on Varga's feet. I was able to swim straight past a whole group.

JONNY

I settled into the top five and Alistair settled on my feet. What a great domestique job I did for him there. I dragged him round the whole swim.

ALISTAIR

I could have swum alongside him, but it would have made it harder for both of us. I let him go in front.

It was actually a very clean swim. There was almost no naughty business, but that was partly because we were sensible. Alexander Bryukhankov started to my right and went out hard so I settled in just behind his feet and Jonny came across to mine. Had that been anyone but my brother I would have kicked them in the head to keep them away; but if I'd been anyone else he would have swum over the top of me. And because we were on the outside, we were away from the madness.

JONNY

Coming out of the water into the deafening noise I felt good. Into the first transition, swim-hat and goggles into the box, wet-suit thrown in too, helmet on and strap fastened, bike grabbed, run run run to the mount line, on to the bike and push on.

To me it felt like every transition one I'd ever done. It didn't even cross my mind that something might have gone wrong.

There was no announcement; no one in the stands, not even Mum and Dad, had the faintest idea. The first clue came when a small 'P' appeared next to my name on the official information system. 'P' for penalty.

A board was held up as we sped past on the bikes with the number 31 written on it. Initially I assumed it was my brother. I hadn't done anything wrong, so how could it be me?

I cursed. Then I looked down at my right arm: 31. And cursed again, and again.

It meant that I would have to stop for fifteen seconds at some point during my run. Just stand there, breaking my rhythm, while others might fly past me.

Penalties are often given for not putting your swim gear into the box by your station. I knew I was fine there, as I'd made a point of putting everything perfectly into mine. I put it in, checked. I put my helmet on, checked again. All good.

I had even made a point of saying to Alistair before the race: 'No matter what you do, make sure you don't get a penalty.'

As we flashed past one of the coaches I shouted, 'What have I done wrong?' He radioed back to coach Malcolm. As I came past Ben Bright, waiting on another part of the course, he held up the board to give me my answer: 'MOUNT LINE'.

I still haven't seen the footage that supposedly shows my feet leaving the ground before that line. But Malcolm has, and it is marginal. There is a still shot they showed him which apparently proves it, but they wouldn't show him the whole video from that angle, so we have no idea how many others might have done it too.

I had always thought that as long as you'd crossed the mount line with your front wheel you were okay, but no – you must be entirely over the line. However, the mount line has never been that thick before. I wasn't deliberately trying to get on early, and it's not like I gained any advantage whatsoever, not even a tiny one.

My first reaction was simple. 'For fuck's sake!' Then the logic kicked in. Who can I beat by fifteen seconds? Right. Alistair, probably not. Gomez – well, I ran twenty seconds faster than him in Kitzbühel last month, pretty comfortably – so, yes. I'm fitter than that now too. Bryukhankov? Yes.

Now my brain began to process it. Maybe fifteen seconds isn't so much. This could actually be liberating, because now I don't have a choice – I'll just have to run hard. And then anger again: 'Screw you, ITU! You don't want us to come first and second anyway, and we're still going to do it.'

All this happened within lap two of the bike. On lap three the panic set in.

What if I now come fourth by two seconds? What happens if I miss out on silver by fourteen seconds?

The irony of it didn't hit me till later: Jonny, the Brownlee brother obsessed with timing and punctuality, had been penalized for being too early.

ALISTAIR

Right at the start of the bike we made a small break of five, which was ideal. If we stayed away it was perfect, because we had blown the field apart, and we knew that two of the group couldn't run as fast as us; if we didn't, the pursuing pack would have had to work their balls off to haul us in, and so they would have far less left in their legs for the run.

Even when we were caught, we looked around and realized that there were only twenty-two of us in the pack. You rarely get a group that small. We knew, too, exactly how we were going to ride it with Stu Hayes and Varga, and that was just as we had been drilling it in St Moritz throughout July: single line, thirty-second turns on the front. We weren't smashing it, but we were doing enough to make the pursuers suffer, and we were making sure Gomez pulled his turns too.

Under Wellington Arch, along Constitution Hill, looping past Buckingham Palace. So many potential good runners were out of the equation. With each minute that passed, we were eliminating another possible hazard and making the odds shorter and shorter in our favour.

You might wonder, since we are probably the strongest runners, why we didn't just take it easy on the bike and let our run do the business. Well, that would certainly work five or six times out of ten. But by hurting people on the bike you're immediately upping those chances to eight or nine out of ten. And that's what you want to do in the Olympics: make the race your race.

There was only one short section of the course where the noise dropped away enough for us to be able to shout instructions and support to each other, and that came as you went through the transition area and then looped left over the bridge across the Serpentine. There were no spectators on the bridge, but as soon as you hit the shoreline the cheering hammered you again.

You had almost no time. I heard Jonny shout, 'Fucking hell – I've got a penalty!' Back into the deafening noise, back into our own worlds. The next lap, the next tiny window: 'Don't worry, Jonny. Relax. You'll be fine.' Back into the tunnel of noise. Now Stu Hayes is back with us. 'Ride hard, Stu. We can't let them catch us now.'

Ride hard Stu did. He performed that domestique role to perfection. Now there could be no more questions about his selection, no more questions about British Triathlon's decision to go with that role. He kept the pace fast, he kept the pack in order, he kept it in ideal shape for us. We owe him a huge amount.

Towards the end I even made a cheeky little break of my own. I'd noticed that Stu was starting to suffer and that a few attacks were starting to go, so I went out alone to take the pace out and give them something else to worry about. If I got away, brilliant; if I didn't, they'd have to chase me down, and that would hurt them. And that's exactly what happened.

JONNY

Once again, the practical part of the brain engaged. I would have to serve this fifteen-second penalty somewhere on the run, at the end of one of the four laps. But when?

Ben Bright held out another board: 'TAKE PENALTY 1st LAP'. Okay. I'll take it at the end of the first lap. That way we could go off hard, open up a ten-second lead, let them work hard to catch and then chase them down as they tire. It'll be just a little break.

As we ditched the bikes and slipped on our running shoes in transition two, I made a vow: right – I'm going to smash this bloody run now.

Alistair, Gomez and I went away. And then, as I felt the strong headwind in my face and looked behind at the large chasing pack, I began to recalibrate. If I stop now and have to run on my own they'll catch me. Let's keep this going.

And it kept going. Second lap, same group, same wind. Gomez was still with us. In Kitzbühel I had dropped him really early on without even trying. Here I kept glancing over my shoulder, knowing we were running fast, knowing we were destroying the athletes behind us, yet he was still there. 'Piss off! Drop off! Go away!'

ALISTAIR

I was surprised that Gomez was still with us. But I wasn't worried.

When you race against someone as often as we have raced Gomez, you get to know how they're running even when they're hidden behind you – by the sound of their breathing, by the rhythm their feet make on the tarmac. Not this time. You couldn't hear your own breath or feet, let alone someone else's.

I knew that the first lap was really fast. How could Gomez still be there? How could Jonny seem to be dropping back now? Usually that happens only right at the start or right at the end. It told me I was piling on the pressure.

I was aware that Gomez doesn't have a huge kick in his locker. You're conscious that he will want to put in a big surge around the 4 and 5 kilometre mark, and that decided my tactics. Not once was I scared; I was actually looking forward to a good battle, to a true race, just as we had fought on the Gold Coast all those years before. And my legs felt good. Really good.

Going down the hill towards the Serpentine Lido, I was conscious a small gap had opened up behind me. Right, Alistair – let's put in a big effort here, let's break him, let's win this . . .

JONNY

Third lap. Good gap. Don't want to get to the end of the final lap and have to stand there, finish line in sight, and wait and wait.

Now. I'll take it now.

I ran into the boxed-off penalty area. Physio Emma was there. 'Look at me, Jonny! Calm down! Look at me!'

Suddenly it was quiet. I looked up. Only eight seconds to go. 'Bloody hell, this is going fast.'

As I stared, time seemed to slow. Each second now crawled. Come on, come on . . . Four. Three. If I go early, will anyone notice? Two. Accept that this first 500 metres will feel horrible. One. Come on, Jonny. Gone. Go! Go!

ALISTAIR

The noise was so intense with a lap to go that my ears were ringing. We thought we knew what a home Olympics would be like because we had experienced huge crowds and wonderful support in Hyde Park in previous years. But this was mind-blowing, like nothing we could have ever imagined, like nothing triathlon has ever seen before.

That bridge was the only tiny segment when you felt on your own, the tarmac under your feet rough and uncomfortable and the gradient sloping up enough to be cruel. But it was a brief torment before the crowds enveloped you once again and carried you onwards.

As the cheering supporters slid by in waves, I could, strangely, pick out faces and familiar groups – school friends I hadn't seen for six years, voices from the past shouting out, vests of our old club Bingley Harriers. Our parents, my girlfriend, Flick, and our agent, Richard, were in the main stand on the north side of the lake, right by transition and the finish line, but for once the grandstand was the quietest place on the course. From now on, I was in a world of my own.

JONNY

I actually tripped coming out of the penalty box. I nearly blew the whole thing all over again. But within a few paces I felt better than I'd feared. Maybe, I thought, this break has actually done me good.

When I entered the box I knew I had twenty-seven seconds over the French guys battling for fourth. So that's twelve now. Okay. Let's say I've slowed down a bit. Let's call it ten seconds.

Right. What time would I be happy with for this final 2.5 kilometres? What gap do I need going to the first time-check with coach Glen, a third of the way round that final lap – eight seconds?

I knew I had to run hard. I knew that if the French guys hadn't eaten into my lead by halfway round, they would stop believing it might happen. So hard I went.

I drive past Glen. Up goes the board: '16 SECONDS'. Sixteen seconds! I'm pulling away again!

I keep it going. One kilometre to go. I can't let them catch me here. They can't catch me here. But will I even be aware of them coming? Usually you can hear a rival's footfalls or their breath rasping, but the support from the British crowd was unrelenting. I couldn't hear a thing. You can normally look back over your shoulder, but the crowds were so dense, leaning so far over the barriers, that I couldn't see anyone.

ALISTAIR

I glanced back. Gomez was gone. With two kilometres to go the shout came from one of the coaches: 'Seven seconds!' Seven seconds to defend over 2,000 metres? Okay, I know I can do that, but keep pushing – four seconds a kilometre is too easy to lose.

I went hard along the back straight for the final time. The thought started creeping in, shouting louder then even louder – I'm going to be Olympic Champion, I'm going to be Olympic Champion . . .

Push it away, Alistair, don't get ahead of yourself.

Still the gap was growing, but I was desperate not to mess up. Two years before on that exact stretch of road I had collapsed, within hailing distance of the finish line. This time I would take no chances. I must keep a clear head and stay balanced on that fine line between going hard and going so hard that I risked losing it all.

JONNY

Only 800 metres to the line. Don't come fourth now. Don't come fourth. Only 500 metres. Come on – it's only 500 metres. It can't go wrong now . . .

ALISTAIR

I'm on the finishing straight. Everything is blurring – I've been pushing it so hard that I'm beginning to lose it. My consciousness is slipping. The line is upon me.

I stop, a Union flag around my shoulders. I look back. No Gomez. No one else.

Arms up. Exhaustion. No emotions, just exhaustion and confusion. How do I hold this flag? Is it the right way round? Why can't I hold it so it flutters? It's getting caught on my shoulders. The line. I'm across the line. I'm Olympic Champion. I'm Olympic Champion!

JONNY

Only 400 metres. Give it everything. Only 300 metres. As fast as you can. Only 200 metres. No breaths in my ears. No rivals on my shoulders. Only 100 metres. I've made it. Clenched fist. I've made it.

Gold and bronze. Thank God it's over . . .

After the Storm

JONNY

I crossed the line and fell into Alistair's sweaty arms. 'We've done it,' I mumbled. 'We've done it.'

There was so much pain, and so much relief that it was over, that celebrating was the last thing either of us could manage. We were taken into a small Portakabin to wait for the medal ceremony, and my world began to fall apart.

The officials were on full official duty. 'Podium tracksuits on, please.' I was barely aware of what they were saying. The heat was intense, the room windowless. I began to feel ill, then bad, then awful.

I tried to put the tracksuit on, feeling as if I was moving through glue. Sweat was pouring off me. I was faced with a flight of stairs, the medal ceremony about to happen, and there was only one thing I could do: hit the deck.

There was vomit, a lot of it through the nose, and there was ice being wrapped around me. At one point they pulled a black cloth off the photographers' position and tried to cover me with it, which concerned some people who were watching as that's what they do at the Grand National when they're about to shoot an injured horse.

For an hour I was unable to stand, let alone walk. A wheelchair was brought, much to my embarrassment. Even more to my embarrassment, when I was taken into the doctor's room they wedged a thermometer up my backside. It wasn't quite what I'd imagined the moment of Olympic glory might feel like.

ALISTAIR

Mum, as always, was panicking. Dad, his professional interest piqued, seemed mainly concerned with how impressive a resuscitation room it was. I wasn't too worried. I'd seen Jonny like that before, and I knew he would be okay. Of more concern was that he might have to stand on the Olympic podium wearing just his shorts; his special tracksuit was soaked with sweat and covered in blue vomit.

On to the podium.

I looked around. This was supposed to be the best moment of my life, but what did it feel like? It felt like every other podium I'd been on. The same people were presenting the medals who present them at World Series events; the carpet was the same familiar blue. I wanted to log all the tiny details in my mind for evermore, but nothing stood out, and nothing wanted to stick.

JONNY

I just wanted the medal ceremony to be over. I felt so rough that I was unable to think about savouring this special moment. I wasn't sure what to do. Should I bow? Should I smile? Should I bellow the National Anthem in my horribly tuneless way, or should I just mouth it? I went for the latter. No one needed to hear me ruin the anthem at that point.

Small random details. The medal felt huge and heavy. The flowers seemed puny and rather pointless.

It was almost something of an anti-climax. I was so shattered that my overriding desire was to just go home and lie down. Looking back now I find that somewhat upsetting. Couldn't I have enjoyed it all a little more?

ALISTAIR

There was almost no pause in the madness to allow us to celebrate. We were taken back to the hotel by the army lads – an excellent escort – and at last saw Mum and Dad, Flick, Malcolm and Richard Downey and others. But it was all so brief. A shower, some food, and then on to the merry-go-round of interviews and appearances that would define the next surreal week. GB tracksuit on, gold medal in pocket.

Mum and Dad kept it simple: 'Well done, boys.' I think they were just relieved it was all over. Before the race they had sent us a series of short, slightly anxious texts. 'Proud of you.' 'You're still young.' It felt like they were trying to protect us in case it all went wrong. Younger brother Ed? He looked bored, completely unimpressed with it all.

It was close to eleven p.m. by the time we could start to relax, and even then I found that being Olympic Champion didn't seem to mean much. We dashed to a pub near our hotel for a celebratory pint, only to be told that they'd just rung the bell for last orders. 'But I've just won an Olympic gold medal!' 'Doesn't matter. We're closing.'

That, clearly, was not going to stop us. We piled down to a celebrity cocktail bar with Varga and forty random Slovakians in tow. They were all wearing tatty shorts and yellow 'VARGA!' T-shirts, and they tore the place to shreds. It didn't matter that Ian Thorpe was in there, or that this was supposedly one of the coolest places in London. It was carnage.

JONNY

It was madness, some of it good, some of it bad. Chatting with Mo Farah about his double golds, there was amazement on both sides. 'How do you run ten kilometres with a fifty-two-second last lap?' 'How do *you* run ten kilometres that fast after riding a bike and swimming fifteen hundred metres?'

Our social circle became increasingly random during that frenetic week in London. Prince Harry impressed me because he knew all about Gomez and how the World Series was going. The Duchess of Cambridge knew slightly less about triathlon but was still pleasant, while Deputy Prime Minister Nick Clegg looked everywhere else in the room while talking to me and then walked off halfway through our conversation.

I had the notion that once our race was over we could pile into the Olympics proper, free tickets waiting for whatever event we chose – boxing and table tennis during the day, athletics in the evening. It wasn't true. We managed to sneak into the main stadium to watch David Rudisha blow away the 800 metres world record, but that was almost it. I actually had a ticket for Mo's 5 kilometres final, but I turned it down because I was so exhausted I had to rest, something which will haunt me for ever. I would have seen more of the Olympics sitting at home in Yorkshire than I did living in the Olympic village.

Only later could I start to reflect on the race itself.

Did the penalty change anything? Gomez had already dropped me. That is undeniable. What we don't know is how he would have run if I'd been on his heels for that final lap. He crossed the line twenty seconds ahead of me, so a full five seconds clear even without my penalty. Could I have closed that gap if he'd been in my sights? Did he take it easy once he knew gold had gone, and so would have had more left in the tank had I been closer?

It would have been interesting, because he's the sort of runner who hates having people around him in the final kilometre. Did the stress of the penalty sap me at all? Did those fifteen seconds actually equate to more like twenty-one or twenty-two once you take into account that I had to slow down to enter the box and then start again from motionless? At the same time, my legs had been blowing. I was on the very edge.

My feelings about the bronze changed as the days after the race passed. At first, I thought, bronze! Great! Alistair and Gomez were unbeatable. This is great!

And then the reassessment began. Bronze? I came here for gold. What's bronze? Maybe I could have pushed harder. I know I could have pushed harder. Why didn't I push harder?

The sober reality is that I did as well as I possibly could. Your brain can never accurately recall the physical pain you have experienced. Your reaction the instant after the race is always the most accurate, and you saw what happened to me then. And I think I dealt with the stresses of the penalty pretty well. I absorbed it. I made my own tactical decisions, and I made the right ones.

I have no problem, either, with being beaten by Gomez. He is a great triathlete. He should have taken gold in Beijing, and he is a nice guy. But he shocked me with how fast he was in London. That was the fastest he has ever run. None of us saw that coming.

As the weeks went past I was aware too of how serendipity had favoured us. To have a home Olympics in a year when both of us were close to our peaks as athletes was the most enormous good fortune. Had London come four years earlier we would have been too young, and the profile of the sport in 2008 was nowhere near where it was in 2012.

ALISTAIR

You think and think and think about the Olympics. Then, so quickly you cannot possibly take it all in, they've gone. It's like Christmas Day when you're a kid; you spend weeks obsessing over it, and when it arrives it's a good day, but not extraordinarily different to every other one. And then you wake up and it's over. You find yourself thinking: was that it?

The strangest thing was not being quite sure how I was supposed to feel. There was so little emotion there, and I expected more.

I expected to feel wonderful, or maybe to exist in a constant state of ecstasy. Instead, nothing had changed. I was exactly the same person, wearing the same clothes, with the same ambitions and characteristics. I was an Olympic Champion, but what did that really mean? What did that do?

Others changed more than I did. I noticed that I was treated differently. Walking down the street, people stared at me and then did a double-take. Everyone stared. Sometimes I enjoyed it; I could walk into any bar or nightclub, straight to the front of the queue, and drink for free all night long. But it was still disconcerting.

We moved into the athletes' village thinking life would be sweet. Instead everything became more difficult. Everywhere we went people wanted their photo taken with us – other athletes, the Gamesmakers, security staff. The first few times it's great. The next few times it's fine. But when you can't walk anywhere without it happening, you can start to resent it a little. If we had spent ten minutes with everyone who wanted it, we would still be there.

We must have done twenty television interviews in a row on

one day. You begin craving even an hour to yourself, an hour of normality, although we did enjoy the questions about how Yorkshire's medal tally was better than Australia's.

We began to fantasize about being back in our Bramhope house, sitting on the sofa watching TV, even as we were aware that as soon as we were doing that we would want to be back at the Olympics. Achieving your life's great goal is meant to lead to fulfilment and inner peace; sometimes, I just felt tired and confused.

When we used to go running in the Chevin Country Park we would never be recognized. After the Olympics it was the opposite – constantly recognized everywhere we went. I hoped that our success would benefit the sport, that thousands more would be taking up triathlon, and that its profile at the elite level would go through the roof.

Soon we learned how we might be able to stay incognito: never wear your Great Britain tracksuit, walk ten metres apart so people don't see you together, don't stop once or you'll be there for good, communicate to each other via your mobile phone as you walk along so people think you're busy. It's crazy for a triathlete to experience these things, let alone complain about them, but for those giddy weeks, that was our new reality. It made me feel better that Jonny and I experienced it together, that it wasn't just me on my own.

We had built up towards the Olympics for so long that there was a spooky emptiness about the first few weeks afterwards. I felt at times as if I had fallen into a giant crater.

I knew too that – at just twenty-four years old – there was a real danger that life, and racing, and triathlon, would in some ways never be this good again. How could we ever better winning the ultimate prize in our own country, in front of the noisiest, most passionate support we would ever experience? If we couldn't enjoy this, how could we enjoy anything else? I didn't think for a moment that the rest of my life would be a let-down; it was more that it was utterly fantastic to have been there at the heart of it all, and for it all to have gone so well. My injury had made me doubt for a long time that these could be my Olympics. That they were could never leave me feeling less than delighted.

Jonny has talked about feeling lucky. I found myself reflecting on all the hundreds of unconnected decisions that had taken us to this point, all the tiny turns of fate – Dad not taking that job in Northallerton, us growing up round the corner from Triangle triathlon shop, Mr Kingham at Bradford Grammar letting us out of school to run at lunchtimes, Coz Tantrum allowing two skinny lads to train with her swim group at City of Bradford.

Only at home did we become aware of how many people cared, how many lives we had connected with. Letters kept arriving from the least expected places. We heard about middle-aged men who had decided to buy bikes, having never ridden before. We even received an anonymous letter from an eighty-nine-year-old man, telling us the Olympic triathlon was the greatest thing he'd ever seen, and that he wanted to thank us for our 'brilliant efforts'. Inside the envelope were two £10 notes. 'I don't have very much money, but I want you to have this. And I'm not including my name, so you can't trace me.'

JONNY

The Olympics had one unexpected side effect: they brought us closer together as brothers. There had been so much stress around us in the build-up. Some of the people close to us were looking for trouble – trying to help us, but in the process creating problems. I think we realized that we both needed our relationship, and we both enjoyed it.

That was a good thing, but not everything that came out of that extraordinary sixteen days was.

This will sound awful. But I found everything about the Olympics a tiny bit of a let-down. It's not the fault of the Games. It's that your own expectations are so high. We are so used to the triathlon bubble. You get recognized at a race, do a few media commitments there and then you're away back to normality. At the Olympics everything is supersized. You're recognized by more people. You're wanted for more interviews.

Life had undeniably changed. When it was time to head back north to Yorkshire, we could throw away our train tickets: a local company offered us a free helicopter to take us from London to Leeds-Bradford airport. That was weird and wonderful enough by itself. When the helicopter landed, we then had a welcome party of hundreds of local schoolchildren. Back at the house there were still more, and banners were strung out along the street.

With a little time and physical distance I could see that what we had experienced was pretty incredible. But in the moment I often found it uncomfortable. I wanted to spend time with Mum and Dad, and there was no chance. And they couldn't believe we were so busy that we couldn't spare an evening to see them.

I began thinking about the future, about upgrading bronze to gold in Rio in 2016.

How would the experience compare? We had arrived in London riding a wave of home support and hype. Images of us were plastered around almost every phone box in the capital. Brazil could never be the same.

When you're twenty-two, four years can feel like a long time.

I knew I would still be racing triathlon. But maybe I would mix it up. Maybe I would focus on cross-country running one winter, or work on my 10 kilometre time on the road. I loved my sport. But I would need to stay fresh, and that would mean fresh challenges. Moving into my own house felt like a new start. And that was a welcome one. More space, more chance for me to grow up, more chance to shape my future.

ALISTAIR

Straight after the Olympics I mentioned that I might try to qualify for one of the England 10 kilometre slots at the Commonwealth Games in Glasgow in 2014. I will always be a triathlete, and I want to defend my Olympic title in Rio, but I knew that I couldn't keep everything exactly as it had been for another four years. By challenging it on the track I could give myself a new goal. Although, knowing me, I would sustain a nightmarish injury every winter until the Olympics and face the usual desperate race against time to be fit.

I knew it was a good thing that Jonny was going to move into his own place. Someone asked me if I thought it would weaken our relationship, but I expected it to do the opposite. We would still train together, just not all the time. We would carry on spending huge amounts of time together, but also have space to be with partners or other friends. Change is a good thing, and I believe you should embrace it.

Someone else asked me something even more fundamental: had either of us ever resented being identified so closely with the other, or being seen as one of the Brownlee Brothers rather than as an athlete in our own right?

There was another simple answer: never.

JONNY

Alistair was Olympic Champion. But I still had another title to tilt at in 2012: the world title.

My results earlier in 2012 in San Diego, Madrid and Kitzbühel had put me in a dominant position. If I could race to form in the final race of the season, in Auckland at the end of October, I would succeed my brother at the top of the tree.

Part of me didn't care. The triathlon at the Olympics was meant to be the race that changed everything. It had changed a lot, but it hadn't made me the best in the world. To me, neither would becoming world champion. Nothing mattered more than the Olympics. Was there really any point in me going to New Zealand?

Routine saved me. One morning in September, my alarm clock went at six thirty. By seven a.m. I was swimming in the same pool, with the same training partners, doing the same sort of swim-sets. For everything that had happened, I was still a triathlete, training hard, back in the groove. With the routine came normality, and a deep sense of relief. I am a man of habits and custom. In training I found myself again.

The racing never stopped. For some athletes the end of the Olympics was like falling off a cliff. For me, two weeks after the closing ceremony, it was straight into another big event: the World Series race in Stockholm. London felt a long time back. Of the British Olympic team, only Vicky Holland and I were there. There were none of the coaches, or support staff, or thousands of British supporters. But I came through, holding off Gomez, and that simplified the sums still further: a top-three finish in Auckland, and the world title was mine.

Those intervening weeks were hard. I swam, I biked, I ran.

I tried, and I never gave in. But there was something missing, a tiny but noticeable drop in motivation. So much had changed, yet so little was different, too. I was going through the motions, willing myself to keep it going for just a few sessions more.

To prepare for Auckland the GB team was based in Hamilton, a couple of hours further south. Hamilton is not the most exciting place in the world. It's not even the most exciting place in North Island. It has none of the great Kiwi natural assets – no coast, no mountains, no lakes. It would struggle to thrill anyone, and for me – crashing off that Olympic high, struggling to deal with the aftermath – training became increasingly difficult.

London had dominated our thinking for so long that it was hard to live without it. We had talked about 2012 in interviews for months, thought about so little else. Now I was waking up and thinking, shit – what happens next?

With Alistair at home, I was now – aged just twenty-two – the senior Briton there. There was Non Stanford, Dave McNamee and Tom Bishop, all great triathletes and good friends, and I leaned heavily on their excitement. From that, slowly, my own enthusiasm developed. My parents flew in, along with little brother Ed. I saw Gomez and Varga and Bryukhankov. We moved into the city, I did pre-race interviews, and, without thinking about it, I gradually became ready to race.

I knew, standing on the pontoon, that some of my rivals would have great races and some would have terrible races. It was that kind of race, in that kind of year. The course was tough, the rain constant and cold. Some just wouldn't fancy it. They would make excuses to themselves, even subconsciously: you can't expect me to be at my best in this; it's the end of the season, and I'm tired; what's the point of risking a crash now?

On the pontoon, the strap of my goggles snapped. Don't

panic, Jonny – get the spare pair, line up, push the negative thoughts away. Yes, you're shattered, but so is everyone else. You are the danger man. You are the man they fear.

Into the water, up and on to Bryukhankov's heels. Before the first buoy I was past him, before the second I was on to Varga. End of the first lap, a brief window of air and chat as we raced across the pontoon and back into the water. 'Let's go, Varga!'

He knew what I meant. We stayed away on the swim, and then for two laps of the bike, then three, then four, before the pursuing pack caught us. The effort to stay away had been intense. Varga, weary after a long season, left me to do most of the work. I was tired, my legs heavy.

Into the run. I had to break up the pack. Down to four. Big effort. Down to three. The world title was within reach.

Down to two, me and Gomez, just as it had been in Stockholm, just as it had been behind Al in London. Let's get it done, Jonny.

With 500 metres to go, the two of us were locked together, his right hand crashing into my left elbow with every stride. Just one more effort.

At 200 metres from the finish he went hard. Gomez can't sprint, or at least he never had before. Today was different. For a moment I got back on to him, but with 50 metres to go he went again.

Did it matter? The race win was his, but the World Championship was mine. My first thought, as I staggered across the line, was, again, one of exhausted relief – thank God it's all over.

Al had partied hard after the Olympics, his goal achieved. I had not. The Worlds had always been nagging away at me. At last it was done – the racing, the worrying, the training, the pressure. At last I could reflect on it all. At the start of the season my aim had been for a medal in London. I had achieved that.

I hadn't really given much thought to the World Championships. They had been no more than a footnote to that single race in August.

Was I happy now with Olympic bronze? Becoming World Champion didn't make up for not winning gold or silver. Nothing compares to the Olympics. I understand that now. But bronze felt good. Bronze was perfect for me. The only people to beat me over the past two years had been Alistair, Gomez, Bryukhankov and Riederer. Had a different triathlete beaten me to gold or silver it would have been a different matter. But I was beaten by the very best, and I did everything I could.

In 2012 I did something I had always dreamed of doing. For most of my life I didn't think it was possible. How could I not be satisfied?

ALISTAIR

I always knew that the post-Olympics period would be tough. The whole year had been stressful, and the weeks immediately after London were manic. I went over to Des Moines in Iowa to race the Hy-Vee, triathlon's richest race, but performed terribly – I was weary, out of training, unable to cope with the heat.

It was taking me a while to adjust to the new reality of people wanting to stop us to say hello, of people wanting a picture or autograph. I was still doing the same things, still going for a run, or going out on my bike; what had changed was the reaction to it all. It wasn't all negative – we had people telling us that they had decided to cycle to work or enter a 10 kilometre run because they had been inspired by us; we received hundreds of letters and cards from complete strangers offering congratulations. But it all took time to get used to, and it was tough learning that we had to be nice wherever we went to everyone we met. At times, with the amount of training we do, we will need to eat immediately after a session, but the person who has stopped you for a photo won't always appreciate that. What to you is physical necessity, to them is rudeness.

Then, out of nowhere, a strange end to my strange year. Having started it with a serious injury, worked desperately to get myself fit, won my only full comeback race and then triumphed in the most important race I would ever do, I would end it as I began.

I was due to fly to Brazil in October for a long-overdue holiday, but the morning of the flight I woke up with severe abdominal pain. This is the sort of scenario when having doctors for parents comes in rather handy. I spoke to Dad on the phone; he told me to pop into the hospital where he works for a quick check-up on the way to the airport. Trouble. My blood pressure was sky-high, I felt sick, and on the walk from Dad's office to the specialist the pain suddenly focused on the right-hand corner of my gut. That was it – holiday postponed, in for an operation to remove a dangerously swollen appendix.

On the bright side, the morphine was marvellous. Philosophically, I pondered how lucky I was – that the Achilles tear had happened long enough before the Olympics that I could get fit, and that the appendix had flared up only once they were over. Had the appendix gone at any time in the summer, my hopes of a gold medal would have been dead in the water. It was surreal. In effect I had just a short period of fitness in which I was able to conquer my sport's highest peak. Around that, I was a crock.

JONNY

I finally moved into my new house when I got back from New Zealand. It felt right. There were the simple reasons – we needed more space; I was sick of losing my cycling shoes and gloves in the mess; Al's house had no more room for all our new kit. Then there were the bigger ones: it was good for our relationship, good for its continuation and strengthening. I knew I would miss not spending as much time with him, but we were growing into our own men.

As 2012 came to a soggy end, I thought back frequently to that defining day in August. It felt as though the Olympics had happened in another season, in another time. I would still check my medal occasionally to reassure myself that it was all as I remembered it.

Even the familiar comfort of training felt strange, because that singular aim had gone. The Olympics had been the clearest goal of all. Everything else – win these races, repeat that – could only be fuzzier. And once an aim has been achieved, where do you go next?

The constant, through it all, is Alistair. My house is only a kilometre from his. I will still run with him, still ride to meet him before we join the others in the group. I still pick him up on the way to swimming. At least when he is on time.

ALISTAIR

As winter kicked in hard, that summer's day in August seemed increasingly far away. I wanted to move on from it, but it was almost impossible. Everywhere I went the Olympics came with me; everyone who spoke to me wanted to talk about that one thing. So, on the last day of November, I took matters into my own hands.

It was the night of the British Olympic Ball, a glamorous night of dinner jackets and ballgowns at the Grosvenor House Hotel. Once again Jonny and I were staying within jogging distance of Hyde Park. With a few hours to kill before it was time to shower and dress up, I was tired and stressed, but I knew what I had to do.

I pulled on my tights and long-sleeved top, laced up my running shoes and went back to the heart of it all.

Along the path where the security fence had been, this time with only puddles in my way. Across the narrow road that we had raced along in that sinuous pack of riders. Down to transition, feet kicking through piles of decaying leaves, down to the finish line.

There, in the dark, a cold wind coming through the bare trees, I stood on the banks of the Serpentine and tried to remember it as it had been: blue skies, packed grandstands, the nerves, the pain. Roaring crowds, burning lungs. Chasing Varga through the swirling water, slip-streaming Stu through a tunnel of noise, calming Jonny, holding off Gomez. A small podium, a huge cheer, a heavy medal.

I listened hard for the echoes. All that came back was the far-off sound of a Christmas fayre and the distant rumble of traffic. Nothing else. Just me, the darkness and some ducks.

I looked around, and felt at peace. Time to move on.

Acknowledgements

Thanks, in no particular order, to:

Our parents, Cathy and Keith, for getting us started, for teaching us the love of fresh air and for their ceaseless support.

Ed for his ability to make any accomplishment in triathlon unimportant and irrelevant, and Uncle Simon for introducing us to the sport. Grandparents, uncles, aunts and cousins for on-going support and wearing ridiculous T-shirts for the cause.

Tony Kingham for showing us every footpath in Bradford and teaching us the love of running.

Malcolm Brown for being the 'wise owl' looking out for us all the time.

Jack Maitland for being his consistent self no matter what is happening around him.

Ian Pyper for making us do the hated, but very important, strength and conditioning work, but also being a good friend at the same time.

Emma Deakin for helping to keep us in one piece (physically and mentally). She is a friend and always there when we need her.

Adam Nevins for teaching us the location of every café in Yorkshire and (literally) picking up the pieces when it comes to bike mechanics.

Nath and Josh Edmonson for their unwavering faith in Al's sense of direction and route choice. Our training partners Ian Mitchell, James Boxell, Dave McNamee, Rhys Davey, Harry Wiltshire for putting up with us in all conditions. Friend Sam

Webster because he won't speak to us for a year if we don't mention him.

Alec Duffield for being a great friend and organizing our lives.

Richard Downey for understanding the balance between training and commercial activities, and his straight talking.

Corrine Tantrum for taking us under her wing when other swimming groups made it difficult.

Dave Woodhead for being the most enthusiastic race organizer in the world and for keeping our feet on the ground.

Bradford Grammar School for teaching us that hard work pays off and allowing us to miss school.

Both the University of Leeds and Leeds Metropolitan University, without whom neither our studies nor our sport would have been possible.

Tom Fordyce for asking great questions and portraying our thoughts perfectly while sitting in the comfortable surroundings of the Chevin Hotel.

Joel Rickett and the team at Penguin for all their hard work, advice and expertise.